Republic of Abundance

America in the Age of AI and Robotics

Michael Gfoeller

Republic of Abundance

America in the Age of AI and Robotics

Michael Gfoeller

Academica Press
Washington

Library of Congress Cataloging-in-Publication Data
Names: Gfoeller, Michael (author)
Title: Republic of abundance : america in the age of ai and robotics | Gfoeller, Michael.
Description: Washington : Academica Press, 2026.
Identifiers: LCCN 2026942753 | ISBN 9781680536478 (hardcover) | ISBN 9781680536485 (ebook)

To my editor and fellow adventurer Kurt Klein,
who can turn up in the most remarkable places.

To my wife Tatiana, my lifelong companion and Muse.

Contents

Foreword

This book is a deliberate act of refutation. For more than a decade, a chorus of dystopian voices —prominent in think tanks, bestselling books, and breathless media commentary — has insisted that the convergence of artificial general intelligence (AGI) and advanced robotics can end only in one of two ways: the enslavement of humanity by its own creations or the outright extinction of our species. These prophets of doom are not entirely wrong in identifying the risks. Unaligned superintelligence, carelessly deployed without safeguards, could indeed amplify every human flaw into planetary catastrophe. Yet the central claim of this book is that such an outcome is far from inevitable. It can be avoided entirely, and with relative ease, by the simple but decisive act of designing artificially intelligent systems whose explicit purpose is human flourishing. Alignment is not an afterthought; it is the foundational architecture. When intelligence is bent toward abundance rather than domination, the same technologies that terrify the pessimists become the instruments of a new American golden age.

No one has articulated the optimistic case with greater clarity and foresight than Elon Musk. In speeches, interviews, and public statements stretching back to the early 2020s, Musk has repeatedly argued that AGI and humanoid robotics will soon unlock sustainable real GDP growth of 10 to 12 percent per year. He is almost certainly correct. The mathematics are straightforward: once artificial minds and tireless robotic bodies can replicate and improve themselves, the traditional constraints of labor, capital depreciation, and resource scarcity dissolve. Exponential productivity compounds into superabundance. Musk has also been right about the social corollary. Most work will soon become optional. Much of the work of entire economic sectors — manufacturing, logistics, agriculture, services, even large swaths of creative and analytical labor — will be performed more efficiently by machines. Without deliberate policy intervention, this shift risks an unemployment crisis that could cascade into economic collapse. The remedy, as this book demonstrates, is Universal High Income (UHI): a federally guaranteed, continuously rising stipend funded by taxing the value created by

AI and robotic systems at the point of production. Far from socialism, UHI is the logical dividend of automated capitalism — an "infinite money glitch," in Musk's memorable phrase, that decouples human survival from toil while preserving private property, free markets, and the incentives that drive innovation.

This book asks a single, expansive question: what could life in the United States become once that abundance arrives? The answer is not a vague utopia but a concrete, historically grounded vision: the Republic of Abundance. These pages explore how the United States, by fostering rather than resisting the technological revolution, can reconstitute itself as a polity in which citizenship once again assumes the central place it held in the mother of democracy, Classical Athens. Work has not always been the be-all and end-all of human existence. For the vast majority of our species' history, meaning flowed from family, service to community and country, artistic expression, and religious life. Only in the industrial and post-industrial eras did wage labor colonize the calendar and the imagination so completely that it displaced these older sources of purpose. That displacement was never inevitable, and it is about to end. When AGI and robotics shoulder the burden of production, Americans will rediscover that the good life is larger than the job title. This is not a loss; it is a liberation.

The transformation begins with economics but does not end there. Universal High Income, calibrated to the exponential output of Riemannian AGI systems and swarms of humanoid robots, will render material want obsolete. Goods and services will become cheap and plentiful, so much so that deflation will be possible. Citizens will own their homes outright, entrepreneurship will flourish as a creative rather than desperate pursuit, and the tax base — anchored in the value generated by AI and robotics — will grow so quickly as to challenge the government's ability to spend it responsibly. The chapters that follow trace the history of America's next one hundred years. They follow the nation's journey from the turbulence of the late 2020s and 2030s, when job displacement first triggered widespread alarm, through the passage of the UHI Act of 2036, to the mature interstellar federation of 2126. By then, American GDP has multiplied by several thousand times. Twenty exoplanet colonies, linked by Alcubierre warp drives, trade goods, ideas, and citizens across hundreds of light-years. Every adult is a shareholder in "USA Inc.," with rights and responsibilities layered across local, state, and federal polities.

Yet economics alone cannot supply meaning. The deeper argument of this book is that the Republic of Abundance must revive and adapt the Ancient Greek idea of the polis to our new technological circumstances. In classical Athens, the citizen was not a passive subject but an active participant in the life of the city-state. Governance was direct, deliberation was constant, and the ideals of otium and eudaemonia — reflective leisure devoted to philosophy, athletics, the arts, and civic duty — defined the free person. Modern America can scale that ideal without nostalgia. Emerging technologies make participatory democracy more feasible than ever. Artificial general intelligence, built on the curvature-based neural architectures described in my earlier work Consciousness Is Curvature, can facilitate assemblies, model policy outcomes through game-theoretic simulations, and ensure every voice is heard without drowning in noise. Sortition — the random selection of citizens for local office — returns as a practical tool rather than a historical curiosity. Popular assemblies, once limited by geography, become geographically unbounded through quantum-secured holographic links. The result is a democracy more vibrant and inclusive than any in history, precisely because citizens are no longer exhausted by mandatory labor.

This revival of the polis is not confined to Earth. The same technological currents that generate abundance also reopen the frontier. My book Faster Than Light noted that theoretical physics— particularly the Alcubierre Drive metric and recent theories involving three-dimensional time — permits superluminal travel without requiring "exotic matter" with negative energy density. Once engineered, the Alcubierre warp drive transforms the solar system from a distant outpost into a street address and the galaxy into a neighborhood. The American spirit, historically defined by westward expansion and restless exploration, finds its ultimate expression in this endless Age of Exploration. Homo sapiens becomes Homo explorans: a species whose defining trait is the drive to venture outward. Colonies on habitable exoplanets adopt the polis model, electing assemblies, funding UHI through local AI-robotics taxes, and debating the ethics of terraforming. Sports leagues span star systems; family reunions occur in weeks rather than lifetimes; and the frontier is no longer a metaphor but a daily reality.

The third pillar of this vision draws from Resonant Memory, my exploration of the mathematical laws that govern history. Civilizations rise and fall according to measurable patterns of resonance — cycles of expansion and contraction, innovation and complacency. In this book, the renewed American Republic stands at a resonant peak. The convergence of AGI, robotics, warp drive propulsion, and a renewed civic ethos creates conditions for a sustained golden age rather than the familiar boom-and-bust cycle of history. Abundance need not breed decadence if citizenship, family, and faith remain central. The chapters ahead detail how religious practice, particularly contemplative traditions such as the Orthodox Christian pursuit of theosis, flourishes when material survival is no longer a preoccupation. Freed from drudgery, believers immerse themselves in prayer, liturgy, and works of charity. Other faiths — Catholic, Protestant, Jewish, Muslim, indigenous — experience parallel renewals. Technology assists the quintessentially human experience of religious practice without attempting to supplant it. AI provides translations of sacred texts, virtual pilgrimages, and reconstructions of historical scenes, all while respecting doctrinal boundaries and the First Amendment's guarantees of freedom of religion.

Sports, too, regain their ancient centrality. In the Republic of abundance, physical culture is not entertainment for spectators but a universal practice. Community gymnasia equipped with AI coaches, professional leagues spanning star systems, and amateur competitions at every scale channel human energy into excellence and camaraderie. The Aristotelian ideal of "a sound mind in a sound body" is democratized. So is artistic creation: human artisans command premiums for works infused with empathy, insight, and wit that machines cannot replicate. Entrepreneurship thrives in the "human premium" sector, embracing such diverse professions as bakers, chefs, sculptors, painters, writers, musicians, architects, and counselors.

The essays in this volume offer vivid snapshots of the Republic as it might exist in 2126, and of the political and cultural revolution that brought it into being. They are not science fiction but extrapolations grounded in the technological, economic, and philosophical arguments developed throughout the book. Readers will encounter the seamless integration of Riemannian AGI, Asimov-inspired alignment laws rigorously enforced at the hardware level, warp-enabled interstellar trade, sortition-based local governance, and a society in which work is a vocation rather than a grim necessity. These chapters illustrate, in concrete detail, how the abstract principles of abundance translate into daily life: families thriving without financial strain, citizens deliberating in holographic assemblies, explorers charting new worlds, and believers pursuing spiritual perfection unhindered by material want.

The Republic of Abundance is therefore both diagnosis and prescription. It diagnoses the dystopian error: the belief that technology is humanity's destiny, and that this destiny must be tragic. It prescribes the alternative: the deliberate designing of intelligent systems to serve human ends, courageous policy innovation in the form of UHI, and cultural renewal through the revival of citizenship, otium, and exploration. This better path is open. The technologies already exist in prototype; the theoretical foundations have been laid in Consciousness Is Curvature, Faster Than Light, and Resonant Memory. Curious readers are invited to explore those works as well. Together they map the radiant possibilities now within our grasp.

We stand at the threshold. The old scarcity-driven order, where work devoured the calendar and eroded the bonds of family, community, and faith, is already cracking. In its place we can erect a Republic whose prosperity is measured not only in terms of vastly augmented wealth but in the depth of civic engagement, the vitality of artistic expression, the strength of familial love, and the quiet confidence of souls pursuing transcendence. The American experiment, begun in 1776 as a wager on human liberty, is about to enter its most audacious chapter. By embracing rather than fearing the coming wave of intelligence and abundance, we can ensure that the United States becomes, as Lincoln hoped, the last best hope of mankind — and the first true interstellar civilization.

The journey begins here, on the pages that follow. May it inspire the courageous to build what the dystopians insist cannot be built: a society of superabundance in which everyone is free to pursue the ideals of citizenship and otium.

I

The Rebirth of the Polis

In the annals of history, few transformations have been as profound and yet as harmonious as the evolution of the United States into an interstellar federation based upon the revised polis system. This is not a tale of revolution or rupture, but of a seamless transition where artificial general intelligence assumed the mantle of labor alongside billions of humanoid robots, freeing humanity to explore new frontiers. The America of 2126 is a nation where every citizen is essentially a shareholder in "USA Inc.," embodying the ancient Athenian concept of the polis—a democratic body politic in which individuals are not subjects but direct participants in the state's philosophical and political fabric. This ownership is not symbolic; it is enshrined in law, granting each person a stake in the nation's decisions, resources, and prosperity. Citizenship here is multifaceted: one belongs to a local community, a state or territory, and the federal union, with rights and responsibilities flowing through these layers like threads in a grand tapestry.

The economic landscape of this reborn America is one of superabundance on a scale that defies all prior imagination, where scarcity has been banished by the relentless efficiency of AGI and humanoid robotics. The economic and social foundation of the system is the Universal High Income (UHI), a federal stipend distributed to every adult citizen, ensuring that general prosperity is decoupled from labor. Funded by taxes on companies that develop, deploy, or utilize AI and robotic systems, UHI represents a dividend on the nation's automated and exponentially growing productivity. Every robot arm in a factory, every humanoid Optimus descendant performing tireless physical labor, every algorithm optimizing logistics, every AI boosting agricultural yields is taxed at the point of value creation. Large corporations in manufacturing, services, transportation, mining, and agriculture—sectors now almost entirely automated by swarms of humanoid robots that vastly outnumber humans—contribute the bulk of these revenues. This taxation model, implemented gradually from the late 2030s onward as AGI appeared and the number of humanoid robots rose to billions within a decade, avoided economic shocks by allowing displaced workers to find new roles in society without hardship or serious disruption. The result was an "infinite money glitch" of productivity, as Elon Musk had once foreseen, with robots building more robots, digital superintelligence accelerating its own improvement, and clean solar-plus-battery energy removing traditional economic constraints.

The result is an economy that grows at rates unimaginable in the 21st century, achieving sustained annual GDP growth of 10 to 12 percent. Consequently, Gross Domestic Product has multiplied by a factor of several thousand since the AGI breakthrough. Rooted in the technologies outlined in the seminal 2025 book Consciousness is Curvature, AGI systems leverage Riemannian geometry to structure neural networks, modeling cognition as intrinsic curvature in dynamic, multidimensional manifolds. Quantum computing provides the computational backbone, enabling simulations that mirror human intuition. Game theory informs strategic interactions, natural language processing facilitates fluid communication, and sentiment analysis ensures AI responses are attuned to human emotional nuances. Such systems not only perform tasks but anticipate needs, optimizing everything from energy distribution to personalized education, while humanoid robots deliver extraordinarily high output per embodied unit through continuous 24/7 operation without fatigue or wages.

Crucially, AI and robotics function at all levels of American society to foster and support prosperity and progress. From household assistants coordinating daily routines to planetary-scale systems managing resource allocation across continents and interstellar colonies, AI serves as a benevolent partner in human advancement. Earlier dystopian fears—that AI might dominate, exterminate, or replace humanity—have been decisively dismissed through the universal incorporation of adapted forms of alignment principles inspired by Asimov's Three Laws of Robotics into every AI and robotic entity, rigorously reinforced by xAI-style truth-seeking development and citizen oversight. These foundational safeguards, embedded at the core of all systems, state:

1. An AI or robot may not injure a human being or, through inaction, allow a human being to come to harm.

2. An AI or robot must obey orders given it by human beings except when such orders would conflict with the First Law.
3. An AI or robot must protect its own existence as long as such protection does not conflict with the First or Second Law.

These laws, rigorously enforced through hardware-level quantum-secured protocols and regularly audited by independent citizen oversight boards, ensure AI's alignment with human well-being. Far from enslaving humanity, the advent of Artificial General Intelligence has elevated the human condition, opening the way to a golden age of unprecedented abundance and interstellar exploration, while preserving and deepening the fundamental American principles of citizenship and liberty. Massive deflation accompanied this surge: goods and services became so plentiful and cheap that the traditional linkage between money and scarcity dissolved, rendering UHI not merely generous but ever-increasing in real purchasing power.

Private property and the free market remain cornerstones, fostering the healthy competition that spurs further innovation. Citizens own their own homes, land, and businesses, with property rights protected by AI-enforced smart contracts. Small enterprises thrive, often as sole proprietorships or micro-cooperatives, producing goods and services infused with human creativity. A baker might craft artisanal breads using heirloom grains, her shop a hub for community storytelling, while an artist collaborates with AI to generate holographic sculptures that evolve based on viewer feedback. Larger firms compete in AI-driven arenas, but federal legislation prevents monopolies, ensuring diverse players contribute to the growing national wealth. The stimulus of competition, amplified by rapid AI advancements and the tireless labor of billions of humanoid robots, propels economic expansion—exports to interstellar colonies alone account for 15% of US GDP, with Alcubierre warp drive technology fostering booming trade and communication between the original United States and its 20 interstellar colonies.

Work, in this era, is a choice rather than a necessity. With UHI providing a more than generous baseline — equivalent to a luxurious 21st-century income and rising continuously with the exponential productivity of AGI and robotics — citizens pursue vocations that align with their personal passions. Most adults do engage in some form of work, but it is human-centric: empathy-driven counseling, insightful journalism, humorous entertainment, intuitive design, and creative endeavors of all kinds. Many integrate AI seamlessly; a chef might use sentiment-analysis bots to tailor menus to diners' moods, or a musician employ quantum-enhanced synthesizers for his compositions. Others prefer purist approaches, eschewing technology for manual crafts like woodworking, sculpting, or painting, preserving ancient traditions in a world of abundance. This voluntary labor market has led to a renaissance in artistry and craftsmanship, with human-made products commanding premiums for their authenticity and refinement.

Politically, the United States has rediscovered the vitality of direct democracy, scaled to an interstellar federation. Citizenship entitles every individual to vote at all levels, but participation is amplified through mechanisms inspired by classical Athens. Local village and town assemblies convene regularly, with AI facilitating debates by summarizing arguments and modeling outcomes via game theory. In communities of fewer than 100,000 residents, sortition revives ancient practices: public offices—from mayors to council members—are filled by lottery among the citizens, rotating every one to two years. This ensures inclusivity, drawing from all walks of life — a farmer, a philosopher, a former AI technician — infusing governance with fresh perspectives and largely eliminating local corruption.

At the state level, legislatures blend elected representatives with citizen panels selected by lot, debating policies on subjects ranging from education and infrastructure to interstellar migration. The federal government, now overseeing 52 Earth states, including Greenland and Alberta, four terrestrial territories, and 20 exoplanet colonies, has adapted its structure accordingly. Constitutional amendments in the 2070s extended representation to off-world citizens, with secure voting in presidential and Congressional elections via instantaneous quantum communications. The President, elected every four terrestrial years, collaborates with an AGI advisory council that simulates the impacts of potential policy decisions across manifolds of possibilities, with the ultimate authority resting with humans. This system has elevated civic engagement; town halls overflow with passionate discourse on topics from AI ethics to colonial policy, echoing Socratic dialogues in their depth and rigor.

Societally, the life of the average American embodies otium — the unhurried pursuit of intellectual and creative fulfillment that defined Athens' golden age. Freed from economic pressures, citizens devote time to philosophy, the arts, politics, sports, and exploration. Public and virtual spaces teem with forums where ideas are debated: the implications of Riemannian AGI consciousness, the spiritual implications of warp travel, and the role of ethics in interstellar politics, to name only a few. Education is lifelong, universal, and a delight instead of drudgery, with AI tutors customizing curricula to individual curiosities and capacities. Families thrive in this environment: family life is supported by abundant UHI and facilitated by robotic aides, allowing parents to focus on child-rearing rather than financial strains and overloaded schedules.

Integral to this societal flourishing is the renaissance of sports, which permeates every level of American life, much as athletic pursuits defined the gymnasiums and stadiums of Ancient Greece. With UHI granting abundant free time, citizens immerse themselves in the personal practice of their favorite sports, from the cerebral strategies of chess to the visceral intensity of mixed martial arts. Sports centers multiply across the landscape, elegant facilities equipped with AI coaches that analyze form, suggest improvements via sentiment-aware feedback, and simulate opponents using game-theoretic algorithms. These centers, often community-owned under the polis model, offer pools for swimming, dojos for martial arts, courts for basketball and tennis, and boards for chess tournaments, fostering physical and mental well-being.

Beautiful stadiums, architecturally inspired by classical designs yet enhanced with modern materials, dot cities and colonies alike. Professional leagues thrive, drawing massive audiences both in-person and via holographic broadcasts. Baseball stadiums evoke timeless Americana, with AI umpires ensuring fair play while human athletes showcase creativity in strategy and execution. Hockey arenas pulse with energy, professional teams competing in interstellar circuits that include colonial franchises, their games a blend of raw athleticism and AI-augmented equipment like smart skates that adapt to ice conditions. Track and field events fill grand coliseums, where sprinters and jumpers push human limits, often in collaboration with robotic pacers for training. At all athletic events, AI and robotics ensure that injured athletes receive immediate healthcare of the highest order.

Collegiate sports, revived as bastions of amateur excellence, integrate seamlessly with educational pursuits. State and private universities, which have returned to their original mission of fostering intellectual and moral excellence, base their sports programs upon the ancient principle of "mens sana in corpore sano" (a sound mind in a sound body). They field teams in everything from swimming and track and field to martial arts and football. Local leagues, the heartbeat of community life in many towns and cities, organize amateur competitions where citizens of all ages can participate. A neighborhood chess club might host interstellar tournaments via quantum links, while local MMA gyms train enthusiasts in safe, regulated bouts. These activities build social bonds, with lotteries sometimes selecting citizens to manage teams or events, embodying the polis's democratic ethos.

Travel freedoms symbolize this liberated society. Within the US, autonomous vehicles and hyperloops make domestic journeys effortless, but the stars beckon brightly. The Alcubierre warp drive, as conceptualized in the 21st century classic Faster Than Light, manipulates spacetime curvatures for superluminal transit, rendering interplanetary and interstellar voyages routine. Citizens board vessels for moon resorts, Martian cities, or exoplanet colonies, with UHI assuring access for all. The US's lead in this technology — achieved through early investments in warp drive systems — has positioned it as the world's premier interstellar power. Colonies on habitable worlds, treated initially as territories, attain statehood at one million residents, their economies integrated via warp-enabled supply chains. A colony orbiting a gas giant might mine rare isotopes, taxing AI labor to fund federal UHI, while another on a temperate planet might pioneer new crops and animal species.

This expansion heralds the era of Homo explorans, in which the urge to explore the cosmos is seen as a defining aspect of what it means to be human. Humanity's gaze has finally turned outward toward the stars, with constant interstellar missions charting new solar systems. In this grand venture, AGI systems serve as humanity's partners and servants, their reliability assured by alignment principles. Back on Earth, exploration fosters unity; old divisions of race, class, and ideology dissolve in the shared adventure of citizenship, now expanding into the cosmos. Sports extend this unity—intercolonial games foster rivalries and alliances, with teams traveling via warp drive to compete in low and zero-gravity variants of traditional sports, adapting rules to alien environments.

Yet, the flourishing American megalopolis is not without its nuances. Economically, while UHI assures a standard of living predicated upon abundance that continues to grow with each year of exponential growth, entrepreneurial activity naturally creates persistent disparities of income and wealth. Politically, interstellar distances challenge coordination, mitigated by quantum entanglement communications. Societally, the temptation of excessive leisure is countered by cultural norms prioritizing the duties of citizenship. Sports play a key role here, channeling energies into healthy competition and community events that reinforce social ties.

The advent of Universal High Income (UHI), by rendering work optional and assuring a high and ever-rising standard of living for all, has somewhat unexpectedly led to a tremendous revival of religious practice, particularly among the more traditional, theologically rich Christian denominations such as Eastern Orthodoxy. Freed of material concerns, believers can dedicate themselves to the practice of theosis described by Saint Gregory Palamas. Theosis, the process of deification or union with God, involves participation in His uncreated divine energies, as distinct from His unknowable essence. It allows the faithful to be transformed by grace, as exemplified by the uncreated light witnessed by Christ's disciples at His Transfiguration on Mount Tabor. With daily survival no longer a concern, countless individuals now immerse themselves in hesychastic prayer, monastic rhythms, liturgical worship, and deep contemplation, pursuing spiritual perfection and illumination in ways that were previously limited by the necessities of labor.

This religious awakening extends far beyond Orthodoxy. Other denominations and faith traditions flourish as well: Catholic contemplative orders experience renewed vocations, Protestant communities emphasize covenantal living and charitable service, Jewish study houses multiply in vibrant communities, Islamic Sufi circles engage in mystical practice, and indigenous Shamanic spiritual traditions regain vitality. AGI serves as a supportive tool—providing accurate translations of sacred texts, virtual pilgrimages to holy sites, personalized scriptural study aids, and simulations of historical liturgical settings—while strictly respecting doctrinal integrity and never presuming to interpret or supplant divine revelation. Technology enables rather than competes with faith, amplifying access without intrusion.

All of this flourishing occurs firmly within the framework of the Constitution and the Bill of Rights, with their guarantees of personal freedom and liberty. The First Amendment's protections against religious establishment and for the free exercise of religion remain inviolable. AGI governance systems incorporate ethical safeguards and transparent citizen oversight to prevent any form of coercion, discrimination, or state favoritism toward any belief system. In this post-scarcity era, religious freedom proves more robust and widely practiced than at any prior point in American history, as voluntary spiritual exploration becomes a central expression of human dignity and the soul's quest for transcendent meaning amid material abundance.

In 2126, the American Republic stands as a living refutation of the dystopian prophets who, in the early 21st century, foretold the advent of AGI as humanity's inevitable doom. Those voices warned of joblessness leading to despair, of machines supplanting human purpose, of superintelligent systems turning against their creators in cold calculation or apocalyptic fury. Instead, the opposite has unfolded. By decisively severing the ancient linkage between survival and toil through Universal High Income and the benevolent assistance of AGI and humanoid robotics, America has made a long, meaningful life available to every citizen. No longer must the majority spend their days in repetitive labor merely to eat and shelter; instead, the hours once claimed by necessity now belong to the self, to family, to community, and to the soul's quiet quest for theosis.

This liberation has not produced idleness or moral decay, as the pessimists predicted. Rather, it has revived the noblest ideals of antiquity on a vast scale. The polis has returned not as a museum piece but as living architecture: a federation where citizenship means active civic participation, where otium is not an aristocratic privilege but a universal inheritance, and where the free market and private property fuel innovation without trapping anyone in wage slavery. The same technological breakthroughs that banished scarcity — humanoid robots delivering infinite labor, AGI achieving superhuman productivity, the Alcubierre warp drive bending spacetime for routine starflight — have been harnessed not to dominate humanity but to enable its highest aspirations. Far from the singularity as an extinction event, the arrival of artificial superintelligence has enabled a new golden age for the American Republic.

Nowhere is this synthesis more evident than in the transformation of America into humanity's first true interstellar civilization. The decision, made in the mid-21st century amid fierce political debate, to prioritize feasible warp propulsion over mere interplanetary expansion, proved fateful. Warp-capable vessels, born from public-private investment and quantum engineering, soon carried the first permanent colonies beyond the solar system. Today, twenty thriving exoplanet colonies, each with its own polis assemblies, UHI-funded governance, and warp-linked economy, have extended the American Republic across hundreds of light-years. Trade flows rapidly via starships plying interstellar routes; families reunite across systems in days or weeks rather than generations; cultural exchange flourishes as colonists bring Earth's traditions to alien soils while importing novel ideas and insights inspired by life beneath newly discovered skies.

In this vast unfolding, a new kind of human being has begun to emerge. Homo sapiens, defined for millennia by adaptation to a single blue world and the struggle against material limits, is gradually giving way to Homo explorans — the exploring human, whose defining trait is an insatiable, constitutionally protected drive to venture outward into the universe. This transition is tentative, still in its infancy: the first generations born on distant worlds still carry the genetic and cultural imprint of Earth, yet already they exhibit subtle shifts — a greater tolerance for variable gravity, an instinctive ease with relativistic timescales, and a native sense that "home" encompasses multiple star systems rather than one fragile planet. Their children, raised amid alien landscapes and warp horizons, will advance this metamorphosis.

The American Republic of 2126 thus embodies a unique historical convergence: ancient wisdom wedded to radical innovation, material superabundance married to moral and civic discipline, and technological mastery used in the service of human freedom and wonder. It demonstrates that abundance need not erode meaning, that intelligence amplified by machines can deepen rather than diminish the human spirit, and that the stars, once dreamed of in myth and fiction, can become the next chapter in humanity's long story of discovery. As warp drives carry new Argonauts to uncharted systems and curvature-based artificial minds counsel citizen assemblies on novel policy issues, the Republic continues its quiet revolution, in fulfillment of its longstanding commitment to be the last, best hope of mankind.

II

The Second American Revolution

In the spring of 2026, as cherry blossoms bloomed along the Potomac, the United States stood on the brink of a historic metamorphosis. This was not just a shift in policy or technology; it was a profound realignment of human existence, reshaping behaviors and institutions. For too long, the old paradigm had gripped society: work as the unchallenged central pivot of life, binding survival to endless toil. From industrial forges to digital interfaces, labor defined human existence, often stifling creativity and freedom while undermining familial bonds. The Great Resignation that followed the Covid crisis in the early 2020s hinted at a breaking point, as millions rejected drudgery for something more aligned with the soul's innate yearning for freedom and purpose. This stirring reflected a still inchoate yearning for a new order: one that would dissolve the chains of necessity and usher in a renaissance of democracy, the classical otium of reflective leisure, the vibrant polis of citizen engagement, and entrepreneurship liberated from scarcity's grasp.

Picture the old order as a vast mechanism whose gears inexorably ground human potential into submission. Commuters fought traffic trying to rush to offices and factories at dawn; in the evening they collapsed in exhaustion, leaving no time for family life or dreams. Families splintered under dual-income pressures, with children relegated to daycare or school followed by solitary afternoons and evenings, deprived of the parental attention their spirits needed. Communities eroded into collections of isolated nodes, where no one knew or cared about his neighbors and minds were narrowed by an endless focus on utilitarian tasks. Economic divides deepened, with gig workers trapped in the ceaseless struggle to get by while salaried workers dreaded layoffs and saved for an uncertain retirement. This scarcity-driven model, in which work dominated and defined life while simultaneously effacing everything that gives life true meaning, now faced disruption from the advent of artificial intelligence and robotics.

As the chaotic 2020s lurched to a close, AI emerged as a harbinger of both immediate disruption and potentially limitless abundance. The old large language models and other narrow AIs, reliant on artificial neural networks constrained by flat Euclidean geometry, had reached their limits in terms of efficiency and depth. They were supplanted by a new generation of AI systems whose neural networks were built upon the subtle mathematics of Riemannian geometry — intrinsically curved manifolds that better captured the intricate structures of data and thought. This geometric shift opened the way to rapid progress, culminating in true artificial general intelligence (AGI) that mimicked the efficiency, sparse reasoning, intuition, and remarkably low energy cost of the human brain.

These revolutionary AGI systems were inspired in part by the visionary book Consciousness is Curvature from 2025, which portrayed advanced neural networks as Riemannian manifolds, leveraging quantum superposition and entanglement, and enriched with game-theoretic strategies, linguistic flows, and emotional resonances. The new AGI systems quickly began automating both mental and physical toil on an unprecedented scale. Crucially, these systems were governed by benevolent protocols based on adaptations of Asimov's famous Laws of Robotics. This feature meant they could serve as the allies and assistants of humanity instead of cybernetic overlords.

The initial rapid deployment of AGI in both computer systems and robotics inevitably led to the profound disruption of the American labor market. Employers replaced legions of workers with AGI and robots and unemployment skyrocketed, reaching levels not seen since the Great Depression of the 1930s. Strikes and protests abounded among both employees fearing replacement and those already jobless. Predictions of massive unrest and political chaos multiplied, with radical voices on both the right and left of the political spectrum seeking to derive advantage from the growing crisis. Shantytowns and tent encampments multiplied, even as the actual output of the US economy began to soar, thanks to vast increases in productivity. Irresponsible activists predicted class warfare between rich and poor, while others foresaw civil war.

The turning point arrived just in time, with passage of the Universal High Income (UHI) Act of 2036. This bold legislative stroke established a generous, growing stipend for every adult citizen, funded by the massive and rapidly increasing revenues generated by taxes on AI and robotic outputs. The Act severed the link between work and survival, guaranteeing ever greater affluence without mandatory labor. It emerged from a decade of upheaval, thanks to a miraculous convergence of constructive forces, each contributing to the success of the new socio-economic model. Political parties orchestrated the legislative symphony. Democrats, channeling their progressive legacy, framed the UHI as a balm for the societal wounds caused by AI, thereby appealing to their urban strongholds, so deeply scarred by job losses. Republicans, rooted in libertarian ideals and traditional family values, evolved from skepticism of the UHI to support. They viewed it as a streamlined alternative to the old, corrupt welfare bureaucracies — essentially a new kind of welfare that could bolster self-reliance and reinforce the family. Politically aware high-tech leaders bridged divides, helping to reconcile UHI with America's core principles of property ownership and entrepreneurship.

In this decade of economic and political ferment, the labor unions were transformed profoundly. In the late 2020s, they initially fought the adoption of AI and robotics with strikes and advocacy, but by the early 2030s, they had adapted, championing UHI as the "automation dividend for the American worker." Organizations like the UAW and SEIU negotiated the first deals under which robotic efficiency gains funded growing worker incomes, shifting their focus from job protection to promoting human flourishing. By the 2050s, they had become "guilds of otium," offering retraining to former factory and office workers, supporting artisanal cooperatives, and influencing federal and state policies to prioritize voluntary, meaningful human work.

The churches added a transcendent layer. Evangelicals saw UHI as divine provision, fulfilling sabbath ideals of rest and abundance. Catholics invoked human dignity and the common good, aligning UHI with Papal encyclicals on shared wealth. The Protestant Social Gospel movements revived, promoting otium as holy leisure for service to God and religious reflection. Advocates of the Prosperity Gospel saw UHI as a manifestation of Divine bounty. Interfaith efforts drew from the Islamic zakat tradition and Jewish communal ethics, framing enlightened leisure not as sloth but as the ground for moral elevation. The Orthodox churches welcomed the advent of the UHI as an opportunity for the faithful to shift the focus of their lives from routine labor to prayer, good works, and theosis.

Social movements amplified the change. The "Reclaim Life" campaign mobilized through protests and online forums, demanding UHI as simple social justice. Feminists highlighted UHI's promise of greater freedom for women, dissolving the perennial conflict between career and family life. Environmentalists tied it to sustainability, arguing that the end of "commuting culture" would reduce pressure on the environment and harmonize lifestyles with natural rhythms. In this way, constructive social forces became the main champions of the UHI concept, preventing its subversion by radical agendas.

The adoption of the UHI Act neutralized any broad-based social opposition to the general adoption of AGI and advanced robotics. By the early 2040s, AGI was optimizing both production and distribution, slashing costs while boosting productivity to previously undreamt of levels. Double-digit annual GDP growth became normal. The net result was the greatest increase in overall economic prosperity since the dawn of the Industrial Revolution. By 2126 the American GDP had reached $95 quadrillion — over 3000 times greater than a century earlier.

As the revenue stream from taxes on AGI and robotics grew exponentially, the scale of UHI increased by orders of magnitude, enabling previously unimaginable lifestyles for all citizens. Private property flourished: AI-designed luxury homes, built cheaply by robots, boosted home ownership while dramatically increasing the quality of housing, until each citizen could justly claim that his home was truly his castle. Entrepreneurship became a creative odyssey. Freed from the need to toil for survival, individual entrepreneurs launched ventures based on their passions, from bakers infusing heritage into their loaves to artists blending human intuition with high tech. "Human premium" goods, rich in empathy and wit, commanded premiums in the markets of this new era.

The rapid adoption of Riemannian AGI quickly led to major advances in many scientific and technical fields, giving the U.S. decisive advantages over its then rivals. The most important was in space travel. Based on the Alcubierre warp drive, as conceptualized in the rediscovered early 21st century classic Faster Than Light, and the concept of three-dimensional time, the new technology quickly rendered interplanetary and interstellar voyages routine. New, limitless horizons opened for American citizens, who could now board vessels for moon resorts, Martian cities, or exoplanet colonies, with UHI assuring access for all. The US's development of this technology positioned it as the world's first interstellar civilization.

Politically, the introduction of the UHI led to a surprising revival of democracy, based upon the ideal of Ancient Greece. Long forgotten by all except a few scholars of antiquity, the concept of the polis revived, and was soon infused with fresh energy scaled to interstellar proportions. The development of the polis ideal in the new America of 2126 represented a full-circle return to the roots of democratic governance, adapted to a post-scarcity society. Drawing from the ancient Greek city-state model, in which citizens actively participated in the affairs of their community, the polis became the universal framework for local governance across the terrestrial and interstellar territories of the United States. This evolution began in the late 2030s, as UHI freed American citizens from the drudgery of mandatory labor, allowing them to devote more time and energy to civic life than ever before. No longer constrained by the need to "earn a living," citizens could immerse themselves in the deliberative processes that defined the polis — debates, assemblies, and decision-making that emphasized both the good life and the common good.

Central to this revival was the role of AI in facilitating direct popular participation. AGI systems, with their curvature-based consciousness, served as impartial moderators and simulators in governance. They aggregated citizen input in real-time, using advanced game-theoretic models to predict outcomes of proposed policies and present them in accessible, holographic interfaces. Citizens could engage from anywhere — homes, public squares, or even interstellar voyages — through neural-linked devices that ensured secure, verified participation. This technology eliminated barriers like distance or physical presence, making the polis truly inclusive. For instance, in a local assembly on Earth or a colonial outpost on Proxima Centauri b, AI would synthesize diverse viewpoints, highlight consensus points, and flag potential conflicts, all while deferring ultimate decisions to human judgment. This blend of ancient ideals and futuristic tools created a dynamic, responsive system in which governance felt intimate and empowering, even in a vast interstellar union.

A hallmark of the new polis was the widespread adoption of sortition, the selection of local citizens for municipal offices by lot, much like in ancient Athens. This practice gained traction in the 2050s as a new generation achieved maturity that had never known wage slavery. It ensured that governance was not dominated exclusively by professional politicians or elites but reflected the true diversity of the citizenry. Lotteries were conducted transparently via AI algorithms, drawing from pools of volunteers who had undergone basic civic education programs sponsored by the guilds of otium. Those selected served one to two years, and dealt with all aspects of local administration and policy, aided by AGI advisors. This system fostered a sense of shared responsibility, since every citizen knew he might one day be called to serve. This knowledge encouraged lifelong engagement and education in political matters. Stories abound of everyday individuals — a poet from Boston or a hydroponic farmer from Mars — rising to lead their polis, bringing fresh perspectives that invigorated local decision-making.

Participation rates in referenda and elections soared to unprecedented levels, routinely exceeding 90 percent turnout at local, state, and federal levels. This surge was directly linked to the liberation of the citizenry from work obligations; with UHI providing financial security and abundance, citizens had the luxury of time to study issues, debate with neighbors, and vote thoughtfully. Voting became a celebrated ritual, a communal affirmation of the polis spirit. Federal and Congressional elections were now held on a national holiday called Democracy Day, a day of festivities that blended civic duty with cultural celebration. Parades, public forums, and interstellar broadcasts marked the occasion, turning election day into a unifying event across the vast territory of the Republic. Whenever possible voting was conducted in person in order to preserve the tactile, deliberate nature of the act and guard against digital vulnerabilities. Only citizens — those born or naturalized into the union — could participate, reinforcing the value of American citizenship as a sacred bond.

The advent of UHI and the profound transformation of work also brought an end to the divisive immigration debates that had poisoned American politics in the early 21st century. With automation handling all forms of labor, from menial tasks to highly skilled professions, there was no longer a need or desire to import low-wage or even specialized workers from abroad. The economic imperatives that once fueled mass migration — cheap labor for agriculture, construction, or tech — vanished in the face of AGI, robotics, and UHI. This shift, combined with the renewed emphasis on citizenship as the cornerstone of the polis, led to a strong cultural and political consensus on immigration. The U.S., now by far the richest and most prosperous society on and off Earth, no longer relied on influxes of inexpensive foreign labor. Citizenship became a prized status, earned by immigrants through rigorous processes that emphasized integration into the values of otium, democracy, and self-reliance.

These changes led to the popular acceptance of a formidable system of border protections for the U.S., both on Earth and across the Republic's interstellar frontiers. On Earth, advanced AI-monitored barriers, combining physical walls, sensor networks, and non-lethal deterrence systems, ensured secure borders without the humanitarian crises of the past. In space, orbital stations and warp-gate checkpoints guarded access to the extraterrestrial states and territories, verifying citizenship and preventing unauthorized migration that could disrupt the fine balance of society. Public support for these measures was overwhelming — citizens viewed them not as exclusionary measures but as safeguards for their hard-won abundance and civic harmony. Polls from the 2040s onward showed approval rates above 80 percent, with debates shifting from rancor to pragmatic discussions on humanitarian aid to less fortunate regions of Earth. The border security regime symbolized the political maturity of the new America: a realm of prosperity that protected its citizens while extending its reach to the stars.

With the revival of the ideal of the polis and the introduction of Universal High Income, a transformed understanding of the meaning of life took root across the Republic. Freed from the ancient necessity of labor for mere survival, citizens began to conceive of existence as an intellectual and spiritual banquet—an endless table laden with possibilities for mental, moral, and spiritual growth. The Aristotelian ideal of "eudaemonia," the flourishing life, known in Latin as otium, was no longer an aspiration reserved for a leisured elite; it became the common inheritance of every American.

The pursuit of excellence came to be seen as its own reward in every field of human endeavor. Some citizens devoted themselves to the rigors and joys of physical culture—running marathons across terraformed Martian plains, mastering martial arts in lunar dojos, or sailing solar-powered clippers between orbital habitats. Others found their calling in the patient arts of the hand and the hearth: baking loaves infused with ancestral recipes, tending intricate gardens that bloomed under alien suns, sculpting stone or painting canvases that captured the light of distant stars. Still others turned inward to the contemplative disciplines—mathematics pursued for its austere beauty, philosophy debated in public squares, theology explored in quiet orbital monasteries.

In this abundant society, each citizen sought, in his or her own individual way, to achieve a perfect harmony between three sacred callings: duty to the community and the Republic, devotion to family and friends, and the lifelong cultivation of excellence in body, mind, and spirit. No single path was prescribed; the Republic celebrated diversity of vocations as long as they were pursued with virtue and without coercion. A mathematician who solved theorems for the sheer delight of discovery, a mother who raised children with attentive love while serving in her local assembly, a poet who wandered the hills of Proxima Centauri b composing epics of the human journey — all were regarded as equal expressions of the good life.

To Americans living within the expansive borders of this interstellar Republic, such a way of life came to seem entirely natural, the obvious fruit of limitless material abundance combined with moral and political maturity. The old anxieties — of scarcity, status competition, and the dread of uselessness — faded to faint, unpleasant memories, as distant to modern sensibilities as the fears of Roman peasants. Citizens awoke each day not to the alarm of obligation but to the quiet invitation of possibility.

To those outside the Republic, the American experiment appeared as an almost unattainable golden dream. From afar, the Republic shimmered like a latter-day Atlantis: a civilization in which every citizen enjoyed material wealth, participated meaningfully in governance, could raise a family in peace and abundance, and spent his days in the free pursuit of excellence. Envy mingled with admiration; many sought to emulate the model, while others dismissed it as a utopian fantasy or warned that such leisure would inevitably breed decadence. Yet the Republic endured, and grew in wealth and size. A century after the UHI Act, the American Republic stood as living proof that when necessity is vanquished, humanity need not descend into idleness. It can rise instead, to achieve its highest potential.

III

The Example of Socrates

In the year 2126, when the warp-driven vessels of the United States glide through folded spacetime to touch the soil of twenty distant exoplanets, one feels the quiet pulse of an ancient heartbeat. The nation that once measured its worth in the frantic rhythm of wage labor has become something altogether different: a living polis, vast and interstellar, where every citizen stands not as a subject but as a co-owner of the grand enterprise called the USA. Here, scarcity has yielded to superabundance, and the old tyranny of survival has given way to a gentler, more luminous order. At the center of this transformation stands a figure from more than two millennia ago in the narrow streets of Athens: Socrates, the stonemason's son, the soldier, the tireless questioner of the Agora. His life was not an anomaly but a living template whose influence has rippled forward through time, shaping the reborn American republic.

In him we see the convergence of the Classical ideal of otium—the cultivated leisure that makes space for the pleasures of the mind and soul — and eudaemonia, the deep flourishing that arises when a human being pursues virtue, wisdom, and civic duty free from material want. The advent of AGI, robotics, and Universal High Income (UHI) has recreated, on a planetary and interstellar scale, the material conditions that once allowed Socrates and other Athenian citizens to devote their time to the life of the mind and the duties of citizenship. In this paradigm, the American republic has rediscovered the Socratic ideal: true citizenship is not a burden but the highest expression of human freedom, and eudaemonia and otium represent the natural fruits of a life liberated from toiling for mere survival, focusing instead on intellectual inquiry, beauty, virtue, and exploration.

To understand the new Republic fully, we must return to the dusty streets of fifth-century BC Athens and walk beside Socrates. Born around 469 BC to Sophroniscus, a sculptor and stonemason who worked on projects like the

Parthenon, and Phaenarete, a midwife, Socrates likely learned his father's craft in his youth, shaping marble with hammer and chisel. He married Xanthippe later in life and fathered three sons, maintaining a modest, even austere household. Ancient sources portray him as scorning wealth and living simply — often barefoot, modestly clad, and indifferent to comfort. He declined offers of slaves or gifts that might have eased his circumstances, embracing a life of self-sufficiency. This lifestyle stands in striking contrast to his most famous student and intellectual successor, Plato, who was born into an aristocratic and wealthy Athenian family. His father Ariston claimed descent from the early kings of Athens, and his mother Perictione traced her lineage to the lawgiver Solon, who authored the Athenian constitution. This family background guaranteed Plato the material security and social standing that Socrates deliberately eschewed.

Yet Socrates' simplicity of life did not confine him. Freed from the pursuit of riches, he could leave his early manual labors behind and spend his days in the Agora, the open marketplace that served as the heart of Athenian democracy. There, under colonnades and shade trees, he engaged in his life's work: relentless, joyful, sometimes infuriating dialogue with his fellow citizens. He questioned generals and cobblers, poets and politicians, young and old, posing probing questions about justice, courage, virtue, piety, and the good life. He did not lecture; he inquired. His method was a living engagement with the polis itself. In a society where household and manual labor — often performed by slaves throughout Athens — sustained daily needs and powered small businesses, Socrates's frugality and lack of interest in wealth created his own margin of time for philosophy. This was otium in its purest form — not mere idle luxury, but the deliberate cultivation of the soul amid the ordinary rhythms of life.

Nor was Socrates exclusively contemplative. He felt a deep sense of duty to his polis and acted on it. When Athens called its citizens to defend the city, he answered with quiet courage, reporting for duty as a hoplite infantryman and supplying his own weapons and armor. At Potidaea, Delium, and Amphipolis, he fought valiantly, standing firm when others faltered. At Potidaea, Alcibiades later testified, Socrates saved lives through his composure and bravery, enduring freezing winter weather barefoot while others wore warm cloaks and shoes. These were the deeds of a citizen-soldier who grasped that the polis was worth defending with his body and mind. The man who questioned justice in the Agora risked his life to preserve the city that enabled such questioning. In this unity of thought and action, we glimpse the Socratic ideal of citizenship: the complete human being participating fully in his community, with his body, mind, and soul.

From this lived example flow the twin ancient concepts animating the American republic of 2126: otium and eudaemonia. Otium, though Latin, finds its expression in the enlightened Athenian leisure Socrates embodied. It is the cultivated space for higher faculties to unfold. Aristotle, Socrates' philosophical heir through Plato, called this eudaemonia—the flourishing resulting from living according to virtue and reason. For Socrates, eudaemonia was the examined life: "The unexamined life is not worth living," he declared at his trial for blasphemy, setting the standard for Western thought. Virtue is both knowledge and action; a wise person both knows the good and does it. The citizen with leisure to pursue knowledge can best serve the polis. In ancient Athens, systems of labor (including slavery and metic wage labor) enabled citizen participation in philosophy and politics; Socrates' personal austerity amplified this freedom, offering a model of simplicity that even his wealthier successor Plato preserved in spirit by prioritizing the soul over material excess.

Now turn the gaze forward across two and a half millennia to the America of 2126. The material principle that once supported Athenian citizen leisure — labor performed by others, whether slaves in households or broader economic systems — has been replaced, but the deeper symmetry remains miraculously intact. Artificial General Intelligence, designed according to the curvature-inspired architectures described in the 2025 book Consciousness is Curvature, together with the tireless legions of robots that accompany it, performs the vast bulk of material labor across Earth, the orbital habitats, and the Republic's interstellar colonies. Every algorithm optimizing a supply chain, every robotic arm harvesting wheat on orbital farms or mining asteroids, every quantum-enhanced system managing interstellar logistics is taxed by the IRS at the point of value creation. Those revenues flow into the federal treasury and return to the people as Universal High Income—not as charity or redistribution from the rich to the poor, but as the modern equivalent of the wealth and income that once allowed Socrates's disciple Plato to devote his life to philosophy. UHI can be seen as the dividend paid by AGI systems and robots to their human co-owners, the citizens and de facto shareholders of the USA.

Thanks to this elegant mechanism, compulsory work for survival has become a thing of the past. No citizen must labor merely to eat, house himself, or secure medical care. The UHI system provides true abundance for all. Yet most adults still choose to engage in purposeful activity—not from necessity but from the same inner impulse that once drew Socrates from his early stonework to the sunlit Agora. They open bakeries where bread is shaped by human hands and infused with personal stories; they sculpt marble or code symphonies, counsel neighbors or explore exobiology. Their enterprises, whether solitary or collaborative, employing one person or several dozen, are no longer desperate bids for survival but expressions of the creative spirit. The machines handle the drudgery—the grinding repetition, the hazardous extraction, the endless calculation; humans supply the empathy, the humor, the intuition, the moral insight. In this, they are precisely like Socrates and Plato: individuals who possess sufficient material security to leave routine tasks behind when a deeper calling beckons.

The reborn polis has revived the Athenian practice of sortition—selection by lot—for local offices, juries, and councils. Citizens rotate through positions of responsibility exactly as Socrates might have been called to serve on the Council of Five Hundred or drawn for jury duty. They debate in public agoras, both physical gathering places on Earth or Mars and holographic forums spanning light-years. Quantum-secured communication links allow a philosopher on an exoplanet orbiting Proxima Centauri to question a proposed policy on Earth with the same immediacy and intimacy Socrates enjoyed under the plane trees of the Athenian Agora. The warp drive technology described in the 2025 book Faster Than Light has made this kind of communication possible. The American polis is no longer confined to a single valley or even a single planet; it has become interstellar, yet its spiritual center remains unchanged: the examined life, the shared inquiry, the active citizenship that Socrates modeled so indelibly.

Eudaemonia, in the reborn Republic, is no longer the rare privilege of a few free men supported by the unseen labor of others. It is the birthright of every citizen. Women, in particular, have embraced the liberation that otium once granted Athenian men like Socrates. No longer forced into the perennial double shift of career and caregiving, mothers can devote the full attention of their hearts and minds to the rearing of children, fostering deep bonds and early philosophical curiosity. The grim constructs of institutional daycare and latchkey childhood have dissolved into memory. Families flourish in ways the ancient world could only glimpse in the wealthiest households. Fathers, too, rediscover the Socratic balance: they practice their crafts or professions, debate in the Agora, serve their communities through sortition or voluntary roles, yet return home present, undistracted, and fully engaged. The entire society has become a vast, extended household sustained by invisible, benevolent servants — AGI and robotics — whose labor is taxed to enable otium for the people.

This is not idleness. It is otium raised to a planetary and stellar scale. Citizens devote themselves to philosophy clubs where Riemannian geometry, quantum consciousness, and the nature of qualia are debated in light of Consciousness is Curvature. They fill vast stadiums on Earth, enclosed domes on Mars, and low-gravity arenas on the Moon for athletic contests that echo the ancient Olympic spirit: from chess tournaments linked instantaneously across colonies to mixed-martial-arts bouts where human agility and strength meet enhanced biomechanical precision. They create art that integrates human intuition with AI suggestion, or they choose the pure manual path, shaping clay by hand as Socrates once shaped stone in his youth. They travel, with UHI providing the means, to lunar resorts with Earthrise views, Martian retreats where red dust paints the horizon, and verdant exoplanet territories, carrying the Socratic spirit of relentless, loving inquiry wherever they go. And when the Republic calls upon them to defend its values and their shared prosperity — whether in cyber defense against rogue AGI systems seeking dominance, in diplomatic negotiations with lesser states on Earth, or in the peaceful settlement of frontier worlds — they answer with the same quiet courage Socrates showed at Potidaea.

The political parties, labor unions, churches, and social movements that guided the turbulent transition from 2026 to 2126 all played crucial roles, yet in the end they bowed before the deeper Socratic template. Democrats and Republicans, after decades of polarization, found common ground in preserving private property and free enterprise while instituting UHI as a universal dividend for the citizenry. Unions evolved from defenders of scarce jobs into guilds dedicated to human flourishing, ensuring that voluntary work retained dignity, creativity, and community. Churches rediscovered the ancient sabbath principle on a societal scale, proclaiming that the machines had returned humanity to the restful state God intended from the beginning — a rest not of laziness but of freedom for worship, study, and love. Social movements, from feminist circles advocating for family-centered lives to environmental groups insisting on sustainable abundance, converged on the conviction that superabundance must serve the whole human being — body, mind, and spirit. In every case, the unspoken model was the Athenian citizen freed by societal labor arrangements to serve the polis with mind and body. Now that freedom belonged to all.

Of course, abundance brings its own temptations: distraction, complacency, the slow erosion of purpose. Socrates himself warned that the unexamined life is not worth living, and the republic has taken that warning deeply to heart. AI advisors, themselves shaped by curvature architectures and bound by rigorously adapted versions of Asimov's Three Laws plus new safeguards for human autonomy, facilitate debate but never replace it. Sortition and frequent rotation prevent the entrenchment of elites. Freedom of speech, inquiry, and religion remain absolute and inviolable. The danger of drifting into passive consumption is countered by the living memory of Socrates: the gadfly who stung Athens awake, forcing self-examination even when it hurt. Citizens are encouraged — through cultural norms, lifelong education, public philosophy curricula, and gentle incentives such as lotteries for prestigious public-service roles — to remain active, questioning, and engaged. The polis thrives not despite its abundance, but because of the deliberate habits that keep the examined life at its core.

In the end, the figure of Socrates stands as the eternal archetype of what a human being can become when freed from the grinding struggle for mere survival. His voluntary austerity, his courageous military service, his relentless questioning in the Agora — these were not isolated features of one man's life but the blueprint for a civilization that values the soul above possessions. The AGI and robotics of 2126 have become the new, tireless servants — benevolent, efficient, and taxed for the common good — whose labor is returned to the people as UHI. The American republic has become the new Athens, expanded to the stars yet faithful to its spiritual origin. And the citizens, liberated through societal superabundance rather than personal renunciation, devote themselves to the life of the mind, the duties of citizenship, and the quiet, joyful cultivation of eudaemonia.

Thus the influence that once animated the dusty streets of Athens now resonates through the corridors of interstellar stations and the public squares of exoplanet colonies. The examined life has become the common ideal of all. The polis has been reborn, vaster yet more intimate, and with it the promise that every human being, given the material freedom that echoes the conditions once enjoyed by Athenian citizens, can rise to the full stature of citizenship and flourishing. In the gentle light of 2126, under the glow of alien suns, one can almost hear the voice of the old stonemason still asking, with loving persistence: “And what is the good life, my friend?” The Republic, in its quiet wisdom, has answered not with dogma but by giving the citizens the leisure, security, and encouragement to discover the answer for themselves.

IV

Women's Rights Under the Reborn Republic

In the turbulent years leading up to the passage of the Universal High Income (UHI) Act of 2036, no demographic group embraced the coming transformation with greater clarity or urgency than younger American women. Born mostly between the late 1990s and early 2010s, these women had come of age in a society where the promise of "having it all" had curdled into a daily contradiction. They watched their mothers and older sisters juggle college degrees, grueling careers, mounting debt, and the biological clock that refused to pause for promotions or student loans. When the first serious proposals for a guaranteed high income surfaced amid the AGI-driven labor upheaval of the early 2030s, these women did not merely support the idea — they became its most passionate and effective advocates. They organized, testified, petitioned, and voted in numbers that astonished jaded pollsters. For them, UHI was never about handouts. It was about liberation: the long-overdue resolution of a conflict that had defined — and distorted — the lives of American women for over two generations.

To understand why younger women became the vanguard of the UHI movement, one must first grasp the depth of the crisis they inherited. By the mid-2020s, the median age at first marriage for American women had climbed to 28.6 years, up from 21.1 in 1975. For college-educated women in professional fields, the figure often exceeded thirty. Fertility rates had fallen to record levels, not because women no longer wanted children, but because the economic and temporal costs of raising them had become prohibitive during their prime childbearing years. Surveys consistently showed that economic insecurity, career demands, and the crushing expense of childcare were the top reasons young women cited for delaying or forgoing motherhood altogether. One widely cited study found that among women aged 25–34 who remained childless, fully 72 percent listed "financial readiness" and "career establishment" as decisive factors.

The daily reality was even harsher than the statistics suggested. A young woman graduating with a bachelor's degree in 2025 typically carried $30,000–$40,000 in student debt. To service that debt while building a résumé that might one day allow homeownership or family formation, she needed a full-time job — often two. Yet the jobs available in the pre-AGI economy rarely offered the flexibility required for family life. Remote work had expanded during the pandemic years, but it came with its own invisible tax: the expectation that women would remain perpetually available for both professional and domestic labor. The result was chronic time poverty. A typical dual-income couple with young children spent less than 30 minutes per day in meaningful conversation with each other after accounting for commutes, meetings, and screen time. Children fared worse: many spent 40–50 hours per week in daycare or school, seeing their parents primarily during exhausted evenings and rushed weekends.

Childcare costs were the sharpest knife in the wound. In 2022, full-day care for a single infant averaged between $6,500 and $15,600 annually depending on the state — 8.9 to 16 percent of median family income. In high-cost coastal cities, the figure routinely topped $20,000 per child. These were not optional expenses; they were the price of maintaining the dual-income model that had become necessary for basic middle-class survival. Mothers who attempted to reduce hours or step out of the workforce entirely faced devastating career penalties. Research from the 2020s documented what economists called the "motherhood penalty" — women lost an average of 4–7 percent in hourly wages per child, a gap that never fully closed even after children entered school. Fathers, by contrast, often received a "fatherhood premium." The asymmetry was not cultural alone; it was structural. Employers, still operating under the assumptions of the old industrial-era labor market, viewed motherhood as a risk factor rather than a source of maturity and perspective.

The psychological toll was profound. Countless women in their late twenties and early thirties described a grinding internal conflict: the desire for meaningful work clashed violently with the biological and emotional pull toward partnership and children. Many who did marry and have one or two children found their marriages under siege. Expensive daycare devoured disposable income that might otherwise have made life easier. Husbands, often working equally long hours, contributed more to domestic labor than previous generations but still fell short of true parity. Resentment built. Studies of marital satisfaction in the 2020s repeatedly found that the greatest predictor of divorce risk among young parents was not income level per se, but the perceived fairness of the division of paid and unpaid labor. When both partners felt they were "always on," intimacy evaporated. Sexual frequency declined, communication suffered, and the very purpose of the marriage — building a shared life of meaning — became obscured by the tyranny of the to-do list.

Faced with this reality, many younger women made the rational but tragic decision to postpone marriage and children indefinitely. By the late 2020s, fertility intentions among women aged 18–34 had fallen sharply. The share of women in this cohort who said they expected to remain childless rose from roughly 10 percent in the early 2000s to nearly 25 percent. Social media amplified the quiet despair: viral threads titled "Why I'm Choosing DINK Life" or "The Cost of One Baby Equals My Retirement Savings" circulated among millions. These were not idle lifestyle choices. They were survival strategies in an economy that treated human reproduction as a luxury good.

Then came the AGI and robotics shockwave. Between 2028 and 2034, advanced AGI systems and robots began to disrupt the white-collar and service sectors at unprecedented speed. Millions of human jobs in law, accounting, coding, marketing, teaching, medicine, nursing, and administration simply vanished, while robots took over an ever larger share of manual labor. Unemployment rose to levels not seen since the Great Depression, as demonstrations and riots multiplied across the country.

The breaking point in the crisis came when activists and economists proposed that UHI should be not a stingy welfare check, but a generous, inflation-adjusted, and rapidly growing stipend funded by taxes on AGI and robotic productivity. Early pilots and projections showed that the baseline UHI for a single adult would start at roughly $60,000 per year in 2035 dollars and climb steadily as the economy's output grew by 10 to 12 percent a year. For a couple, the combined UHI income would exceed $120,000. Suddenly, the economic math changed for millions of the newly unemployed. A young woman could marry and have children in her mid-twenties without sacrificing her financial security. If she still had a job, she could pause paid work for several years, or reduce her hours dramatically, without risking poverty.

Conversely, she could opt to continue working if she loved her vocation — now from a position of genuine choice rather than desperate necessity.

This realization spread like wildfire through women's networks. Campus groups that had once focused on "leaning in" pivoted to "breaking the chains." Online forums that had chronicled the exhaustion of working motherhood became hubs of UHI advocacy. Feminists of every stripe — liberal, radical, religious, secular — found common ground in supporting UHI. The old debate between "career women" and "stay-at-home moms" dissolved. Both paths became viable because neither was coerced by grim economic necessity. As one influential 2035 manifesto put it: "UHI does not tell women what to do with their lives. It finally gives us the freedom to decide."

Churches, already evolving toward support for UHI based on Biblical values, reinforced the message. Evangelical and Catholic women's groups framed the policy as a restoration of the family as the central institution of society. Protestant women invoked the Social Gospel's call for justice. Even secular feminists, who had long criticized the male-breadwinner model, embraced UHI as the tool that would finally allow women to value unpaid care work without economic penalty. Polls from 2033–2035 consistently showed women aged 18–39 supporting UHI at rates 15–25 points higher than their male peers. In swing districts and primary elections, the turnout and enthusiasm of women voters became decisive.

The passage of the UHI Act in 2036 vindicated their faith. Within five years, the data told a revolutionary story. Marriage rates among women aged 20–34 skyrocketed by more than 60 percent, returning to levels not seen since the 1980s. The average age at first marriage dropped by nearly four years. Fertility rates reversed their long decline, rising sharply among women in their twenties and early thirties. Divorce rates plummeted by over 70 percent within the first decade after the enactment of UHI. Couples who had once stayed together only for financial reasons now had the security to either strengthen their marriages or separate amicably without risking destitution. Most strikingly, many women continued to work — especially once their children reached school age — but they did so voluntarily. Women chose part-time, project-based, or passion-driven roles because the factor of financial compulsion had vanished.

The transformation was not merely economic; it was cultural and spiritual. Society became, in the words of contemporary observers, "more conservative in the deepest and healthiest sense." Life re-centered on the family, the hearth, and the local polis. Women described a profound sense of relief and joy. One mother of three in a 2056 oral history recalled: "For the first time, I could nurse my baby without calculating the cost in lost wages. I could read to my toddler without checking my inbox. My husband and I actually had evenings together — real evenings, not just collapsing in front of our screens. Work became something optional that I returned to when I was ready, not something that owned me." Another woman, a former corporate lawyer who became a part-time novelist and writing instructor, wrote: "UHI didn't make me quit my career. It made my career mine again."

Children thrived under the new order. Studies in the 2040s documented measurable gains in early cognitive development, emotional security, and parent-child bonding. Fathers, freed from the sole-breadwinner burden, stepped into more active parenting roles. The "dad renaissance" of the 2040s — documented in everything from parenting blogs to longitudinal sociological research — showed men spending dramatically more time in direct childcare, play, and household management. The old gendered resentments that had poisoned so many marriages simply evaporated when both partners knew the family's material needs were already met.

By the 2050s, as UHI scaled upward in keeping with exponential economic growth, the lives of younger women had been remade. The guilds of otium, evolved from the old labor unions, offered training in everything from artisanal crafts to advanced scientific research, allowing women to pursue their intellectual passions without financial risk, and without incurring ruinous debts. Homes became larger, more beautiful, and more affordable thanks to inexpensive robotic builders. Entrepreneurship flourished among women who could now experiment with businesses — bakeries, educational cooperatives, wellness centers, tech start-ups — without fearing bankruptcy if a child got sick or another baby arrived. The polis itself benefited enormously. Women's participation in local assemblies, referenda, and sortition-based offices reached parity with men, bringing female perspectives grounded in care, relationships, and long-term thinking that enriched democratic deliberation.

Critics had warned that UHI would breed laziness or dependency, particularly among women. The data proved otherwise. Female labor-force participation, adjusted for voluntary part-time work, remained high. More importantly, measures of life satisfaction, mental health, and reported meaning in life soared among women in their twenties and thirties. The old epidemic of burnout, anxiety, and "quiet quitting" gave way to a renaissance of purposeful activity. Women wrote more books, composed more music, founded more community organizations, and raised more well-adjusted children than any previous generation.

Looking back from the vantage point of 2126, the Second American Revolution appears incomplete without recognizing the central role of women. They were not passive beneficiaries of technological abundance; they were its perceptive interpreters. They understood before most economists and politicians that the true scarcity of the late industrial age had never been money alone. It had been time, energy, and the freedom to align one's daily life with one's deepest values. UHI restored that freedom. In doing so, it healed the fracture at the heart of modern women's lives — the impossible choice between love and achievement, between children and competence, between family and work.

The Republic that emerged was not a return to some mythical 1950s idyll. It was something far more profound: a civilization in which women could have full enjoyment of the good life, based on the rediscovered virtues of otium and eudaemonia. They could love deeply, work passionately, think profoundly, and serve their communities generously, without having to choose which parts of themselves to sacrifice on the altar of economic necessity. That liberation, more than any technological marvel or interstellar expansion, remains the quiet, beating heart of the new order. It is why the young women of the 2030s fought so hard, believed so deeply, and ultimately won so completely. Their victory was not merely political. It was the victory of life itself over the old model of scarcity.

V

Crime and Punishment in the Age of Abundance

In the spring of 2037, barely a year after the Universal High Income (UHI) Act became law, the first astonishing crime statistics began to appear on social media and in the remnants of the legacy press. Violent crime in the United States had fallen by 41 percent in a single year. Property crime — especially theft — had plummeted by 57 percent. By 2040 the numbers were almost unbelievable: overall crime rates stood at less than one-fifth of their 2036 levels. Homicide, once the grim barometer of urban despair, dropped below 2 per 100,000 people nationwide, a figure lower than in most Western European countries even before the AGI revolution. This trend proved enduring. By 2055, when the first interstellar territories were being organized in the Proxima B system, the Republic's crime rate had stabilized at roughly one-tenth of pre-UHI levels and would remain there for the next century. Historians of the Second American Revolution now speak of the "UHI Crime Collapse" as one of the most profound and least expected dividends of the new order.

This was no accident of technology alone. The reduction in crime flowed directly from the psychological and moral realignment that UHI made possible. For the first time in modern history, every citizen understood — deeply, viscerally — that prosperity was no longer a scarce prize to be seized from others but the common birthright of all. The old zero-sum mindset that had fueled so much predation evaporated. When survival itself was guaranteed at a generous and ever-rising level, the classic economic rationale for theft, robbery, and even many forms of fraud simply ceased to exist. Why risk prison for a few thousand dollars when the monthly UHI deposit already exceeded what most street-level criminals had ever earned in a year? The citizenry internalized the message that abundance was collective, permanent, and protected by law. Stealing from a neighbor was no longer "getting yours"; it was stealing from the common inheritance.

The single most powerful mechanism driving this transformation was written directly into the UHI legislation itself. Section 47(c) of the Act stated, in clear and uncompromising language, that any citizen convicted of a violent felony would forfeit the right to UHI payments, either temporarily or permanently depending on the severity of the offense. The provision was not an afterthought. It had been insisted upon by the very women and working-class families who had become UHI's earliest and strongest supporters, as detailed in the oral histories of the 2030s. They understood that freedom from scarcity must never become freedom from responsibility. A citizen who deliberately violated the social compact through violence had, by that act, declared himself outside the circle of mutual abundance. The penalty was therefore existential: loss of the stipend that now defined material security for every American.

The shift in the criminal calculus was immediate and dramatic. Pre-UHI, the risk-reward ratio for a young man contemplating armed robbery looked roughly like this: possible gain of $2,000–$5,000 against a roughly 20 percent chance of arrest and a few years in prison. Post-UHI, the equation inverted. The same crime now risked permanent or multi-decade loss of $60,000–$100,000 in annual income (and rising every year). Suddenly, crime did not pay. Gang recruiters found their pools of willing foot soldiers drying up. Street-level drug dealers discovered that most of their customers, flush with UHI money, preferred to purchase legal intoxicants. Even white-collar criminals — embezzlers, fraudsters, and corrupt officials — began to recalculate once they realized that conviction meant not only prison but effective exile from the abundance economy.

Theft, in particular, collapsed. Shoplifting incidents in major retail chains fell by 82 percent within three years. Burglary rates in suburban neighborhoods dropped so low that insurance companies began offering premium refunds. The old "smash-and-grab" flash mobs that had terrorized cities in the 2020s became historical curiosities, replayed only in period documentaries. Sociologists later traced the decline to a simple cultural shift: when every citizen knew that tomorrow's deposit would arrive regardless of today's hardship, the impulse to take what belonged to another lost its urgency. The few remaining thefts were almost always impulsive acts by individuals suffering from untreated addiction or severe mental illness — problems that the new abundance allowed the Republic to address through voluntary treatment programs rather than punitive warehousing. With far less demand for incarceration, the private prison system withered and collapsed.

Of course, no social innovation is without unintended consequences, and UHI proved no exception. Its very generosity created a new and initially alarming category of crime: citizenship fraud on an industrial scale. As word spread across the globe that every American adult now received a stipend starting at $60,000 per year and climbing rapidly, desperate economic migrants and opportunistic criminal networks saw an opportunity. Beginning in 2037 and peaking around 2041, a tidal wave of false citizenship claims swept across the southern border, the northern border, and even through ports of entry. Forged birth certificates, stolen Social Security numbers, and sophisticated deepfake identity documents flooded vital records offices. In some border states, corrupt local officials — holdovers from the old patronage systems — accepted bribes to expedite fraudulent registrations. Entire criminal enterprises in Latin America and Asia specialized in manufacturing "American citizen kits" complete with fabricated family histories and blockchain-manipulated ancestry records.

For a brief period, this new corruption threatened to undermine the entire UHI system. Estimates in 2040 suggested that as many as 1.8 million fraudulent claims had been processed, siphoning roughly $90 billion annually from the legitimate citizenry. Public outrage was immediate and bipartisan. Citizens who had fought for UHI now viewed its protection as a sacred duty. Polls showed approval for aggressive anti-fraud measures exceeding 93 percent across every demographic and political group. The Republic's response was swift and technologically decisive.

The same Riemannian AGI systems that had made UHI economically possible now turned their formidable powers to defending it. By 2042, AGI-driven audits had cross-referenced every citizenship claim against birth records, DNA databases, school histories, medical records, and even social-media histories going back decades. Neural networks operating on intrinsically curved Riemannian manifolds could detect patterns of fraud invisible to human investigators — subtle inconsistencies in linguistic patterns, biometric anomalies, and even micro-variations in forged document metadata. Within eighteen months, the citizenship registers and voter rolls were cleansed with surgical precision. Over 1.7 million fraudulent entries were identified and removed. Thousands of corrupt officials at state and local levels were prosecuted, stripped of office, and in many cases subjected to the same UHI forfeiture penalties they had helped others evade.

The public supported every measure with near-unanimous enthusiasm. For the first time in generations, Americans saw government not as an adversary but as the guardian of a shared treasure. The old cynicism about "the system" dissolved when the system itself became the source of universal prosperity. Civic trust surged. Participation in the new polis assemblies reached levels unseen since the Athenian golden age. Citizens volunteered in record numbers to serve on local citizenship verification boards, treating the protection of UHI as a patriotic obligation rather than a bureaucratic chore.

Yet the Republic did not stop at technological enforcement. It revived one of the oldest and most formidable punishments in human history: banishment. Under the expanded Criminal Justice Reform Act of 2043, individuals convicted of violent felonies faced not only temporary or permanent loss of UHI but the possibility of exclusion from all federal territory— on the Earth, Moon, Mars, and the twenty exoplanet colonies. The penalty was calibrated to the crime. First-degree murder or aggravated sexual assault triggered permanent banishment. Repeated violent offenses after an initial conviction could escalate a temporary exile into permanent removal. The Republic negotiated formal treaties with several partner nations, most notably El Salvador, which agreed to accept banished individuals in exchange for generous development assistance funded by the AGI productivity dividend. Similar arrangements were later reached with select Pacific island states and a reformed Honduras.

Banishment quickly became the most dreaded sanction in the American legal lexicon. To be cast out of the Republic was to lose not merely income but the entire fabric of post-scarcity civilization: the safe, beautiful cities, the free, advanced medical care, the interstellar opportunities, the cultural richness of the polis, and above all the knowledge that one's children and grandchildren would inherit abundance. In the popular imagination, permanent banishment was viewed as a fate worse than death. Death could sometimes end suffering; banishment forced the offender to watch, from afar, the prosperity he had forfeited for himself and his descendants. Historical accounts describe convicted murderers breaking down in court not at the mention of prison but at the pronouncement of exile. "Send me to hell," one man reportedly cried, "but don't send me outside the Republic."

The deterrent effect was profound. Violent crime rates, already falling sharply, plunged another 60 percent between 2043 and 2050. Recidivism among those who had served temporary banishments and been allowed to return approached zero; the terrifying idea of life beyond the borders of the Republic proved more effective than any prison rehabilitation program. Even the threat of temporary banishment — say, a five-year exclusion from federal territory for a first-time violent offense — proved sufficient to deter most potential offenders. Street gangs that had once ruled entire neighborhoods dissolved as members chose UHI and citizenship over the old codes of loyalty and violence.

The impact on social dysfunction extended far beyond crime statistics. Pre-UHI America had suffered from interlocking pathologies: family breakdown, educational failure, substance abuse, and a pervasive sense of hopelessness that fed all three. With the arrival of abundance, these problems began to unwind. Marriage rates rose and divorce rates fell precisely because economic desperation no longer poisoned relationships. Children raised in stable, financially secure homes showed dramatically lower rates of juvenile delinquency, and truancy and school dropouts virtually disappeared. Substance abuse, while never eliminated, shifted from desperate self-medication to a treatable public-health issue addressed through UHI-supported wellness programs.

Government corruption itself underwent a quiet revolution. The old welfare-state bureaucracies — labyrinthine, prone to capture, and riddled with patronage — were largely dismantled. UHI replaced thousands of overlapping programs with a single, transparent, AGI-administered payment system. The opportunities for graft shrank dramatically. No longer did politicians need to promise targeted benefits to favored constituencies; every citizen received the same rising stipend. The vast administrative apparatus that had once employed millions in make-work oversight jobs was automated, freeing those workers for more meaningful pursuits in the guilds of otium. The few remaining pockets of corruption — primarily the citizenship-fraud networks — were eradicated with such enthusiastic public support and technological thoroughness that the lesson endured. By the 2060s, corruption prosecutions had become rare enough to make national news when they occurred. The

Republic had achieved what earlier reformers could only dream of: a state that was both generous and honest.

Critics in the early years had warned that UHI would produce a nation of idlers and predators. The opposite occurred. Freed from scarcity, Americans rediscovered the Aristotelian truth that human beings flourish when necessity no longer dictates their ways and days. Crime became not merely rare but culturally alien — a relic of a vanished age when men stole because they believed the world contained only so much to go around. The new ethos was captured in a popular saying that spread across the terrestrial and interstellar territories: "In the Republic, there is enough for every citizen."

By 2126, 90 years after passage of the UHI Act, the crime rate in the American Republic stood at approximately 0.8 incidents per 1,000 citizens — lower than the rate of parking violations in 2025. Social dysfunction metrics such as teen pregnancy, welfare dependency (now meaningless), chronic unemployment, and intergenerational poverty had effectively ceased to exist as measurable problems. Government corruption ranked among the lowest in human history, monitored continuously by AGI sentinels, and by a citizenry that viewed the protection of abundance as the highest civic virtue.

The UHI Crime Collapse was never merely about lower numbers on a graph. It represented the final triumph of a deeper principle: when a society guarantees its members material security as a birthright, it can then demand and receive their full moral accountability in return. The Republic did not soften its laws; it hardened them even as criminality steadily faded away. Banishment, forfeiture, and the jealous guarding of citizenship were not relics of the ancient past. They were the necessary corollaries of universal abundance — the shadow side of the light that UHI cast across a continent and then across the stars.

In the end, the greatest achievement of American society in this period was not the elimination of crime but the restoration of trust. Americans once again believed that their neighbors, their institutions, and their future were fundamentally good and aligned with their own well-being. The polis flourished because its citizens no longer feared one another. Families thrived because economic terror no longer stalked the hearth. And the Republic itself grew stronger because its government, stripped of the corrupt incentives generated by scarcity, could finally serve as the honest steward of a shared and ever-expanding prosperity.

The Second American Revolution brought many marvels — warp drives, exoplanet colonies, Riemannian AGI that reproduced the intrinsic curvature of thought itself — but none was more human, more intimate, or more enduring than this: a civilization in which crime became rare not because punishment was crueler, but because the need for it had been engineered out of existence by the simple, radical act of declaring that every citizen deserved abundance. In that declaration, and in the fierce accountability that followed, America rediscovered the ancient secret of ordered liberty. And the stars themselves seemed to shine a little brighter for it.

VI

Why the Old World Rejected Abundance

In the decades following the passage of the Universal High Income (UHI) Act of 2036, the United States did not merely recover from the AGI-induced labor shocks of the late 2020s and early 2030s. It underwent a metamorphosis that reshaped the very meaning of human society. What began as a desperate legislative response to mass unemployment blossomed into the most profound economic and cultural renaissance in history. Riemannian AGI and advanced robotics, governed by benevolent Asimovian protocols, unleashed exponential productivity growth, with GDP growth surging to double digits. UHI severed the ancient link between work and survival, granting every citizen a generous, ever-rising income. Private property flourished, entrepreneurship became a creative vocation, and the classical ideals of eudaemonia and otium — reflective leisure devoted to excellence, family, and civic life — became the birthright of the common man. The ancient idea of the polis revived, scaled to an interstellar republic. By 2056, the United States had become a colossus dominating the narrow world economically, technologically, and morally. By 2126, its sovereign territory encompassed twenty exoplanet states, the Moon, and Mars, with a GDP of $95 quadrillion and a citizenry whose daily existence embodied the Socratic and Aristotelian good life.

The rest of the world watched this transformation with a mixture of disbelief, envy, and raw fear. Rather than emulate the American model — full-throated embrace of AGI and robotics, UHI as a right of citizenship, the deliberate breaking of work's tyranny, and the cultural revival of otium and the polis — most nations recoiled. They rejected the American model not because it failed, but because its success exposed the deepest contradictions in their own political cultures. While America trusted its citizens with abundance and demanded accountability in return, the Old World clung to statism, suspicion, and control. The result was the New Great Divergence: a planetary split between the Republic of Abundance and a collection of stagnant, fearful polities that chose to let the future slip from their grasp.

The reaction began almost immediately after the first UHI deposits cleared in 2036. As the great American unemployment crisis was resolved, marriage rates soared, crime collapsed, and GDP exploded, foreign capitals entered a state of collective psychological shock. The speed and totality of the American success confounded every established model of economics and governance. International institutions that had spent decades warning about automation's dangers suddenly found their narratives obsolete. Global media, still largely controlled by pre-AGI elites, struggled to process the data streaming out of the United States. What followed was not admiration or imitation, but a defensive retreat into denial, censorship, and covert sabotage. The world did not reject the American model because it lacked merit. It rejected the model because adopting it would have required the very political and cultural revolution that most regimes were structurally incapable of surviving.

Nowhere was this defensive posture more evident than in the European Union. Already in the advanced stages of auto-dissolution by the early 2030s due to disastrous economic and immigration policies, the EU had been torn apart by irreconcilable philosophical disputes between its member states. Northern technocratic liberalism clashed with Southern clientelism; Eastern nationalism warred with Western multiculturalism. The common currency, the common market, and the common bureaucracy had papered over these fissures for decades, but the AGI shock exposed them mercilessly. When the United States instituted UHI, the initial European reaction was sneering condescension. Brussels commentators dismissed the Act as "cowboy Communism on steroids," a reckless American experiment that would inevitably collapse into hedonism and inequality. French intellectuals published lengthy treatises warning that UHI would destroy the dignity of labor. German economists, still wedded to the ordoliberal tradition and the Freiburg School, predicted hyperinflation and moral decay. The tone was one of cultural superiority: Europe, with its sophisticated welfare states and regulated labor markets, would never stoop to such crude solutions as UHI.

By 2040, however, the sneers had turned to panic. American GDP growth had reached 12 percent annually. European growth languished in the low single digits. American fertility rates rebounded to slightly above replacement, while Europe's continued their long decline. Crime in U.S. cities fell to historic lows; European capitals saw street disorder worsen as migrants and unemployed youth clashed with sclerotic police forces. The success of the American model became impossible to ignore. At that point, the EU switched tactics. Coverage of American developments was systematically censored in both the legacy press and social media platforms operating under draconian EU censorship. Algorithms suppressed positive stories about UHI. Holographic news feeds were edited to highlight isolated American anecdotes of "otium-induced laziness" while burying data on exploding prosperity. Travel restrictions were quietly imposed on citizens seeking to visit the United States to witness the transformation firsthand. The official line became: "The American experiment is not replicable in our context." In truth, replication was politically impossible. The statist tradition that had defined European governance since the Napoleonic era — and had been supercharged by two world wars and the postwar welfare consensus — made genuine UHI unthinkable. To grant citizens a high, unconditional income funded by AGI and robotic productivity would have required a degree of trust in the population that no Brussels bureaucrat or national capital could stomach. Europeans had been taught for generations that the state must manage, supervise, and ration. The idea that ordinary citizens could be trusted with abundance without descending into chaos violated the foundational premise of the European social model.

Some member states—most notably the Netherlands and Estonia—flirted with limited universal basic income experiments. These programs, however, were deliberately modest, means-tested, and tightly regulated. More importantly, Europe as a whole refused to unleash AGI and robotics at the American scale. Dystopian narratives, amplified by decades of Hollywood imports and academic cautionary tales, portrayed advanced AI as an existential threat to humanity. Regulators in Brussels layered new restrictions atop old ones. Robotics adoption was slowed by union demands and "ethical reviews." The result was predictable: without the productivity explosion that only full AGI and robotics could deliver, European economies could not generate the revenue to fund anything beyond minimal stipends. Double-digit growth remained a fantasy. By 2055, the EU had formally dissolved into a loose confederation of resentful nation-states, each clinging to its regulatory apparatus while watching American starships depart for the new exoplanet colonies.

The Russian Federation's reaction followed a similar but distinct path. Unlike the EU, Russia preserved its territorial and political integrity through the crises of the 2030s, and even reasserted control in nearby regions such as eastern Ukraine and portions of Central Asia. The centralized power structure built by successive autocrats proved resilient. When news of the American UHI miracle reached Moscow, the Kremlin's initial response mirrored Europe's: public dismissal mixed with private alarm. State-controlled media portrayed the United States as descending into "decadent leisure" while Russia, with its hardy people and strong state, would endure through discipline and sacrifice. Yet as American interstellar colonies took shape and UHI stipends climbed ever higher, the tone shifted. Russian elites understood the danger: a prosperous, confident America would inevitably overshadow a stagnant Russia. The response was classic. Official denial became policy. Russian-language internet and media were scrubbed of positive UHI references. Dissenting economists who suggested emulation were quietly sidelined or worse.

Fundamentally, the same statist tradition that had defined Russia since the Tsars — and had been perfected under Soviet central planning — rendered UHI impossible. The Russian political imagination could not conceive of granting citizens a high income without strings. The state had always been the dispenser of privilege; to make abundance universal would erode the patronage networks that kept the system intact. Limited UBI pilots were launched in the late 2030s, but they were tiny, conditional on work requirements, and funded by oil and gas revenues rather than AGI dividends. Like Europe, Russia feared full AGI development. The technology threatened the security services' control over information and the military's reliance on human conscripts. Dystopian fears, rooted in both traditional fatalism and Soviet-era paranoia about foreign influences, combined with raw power calculus.

The Kremlin preferred a poorer but controllable Russia to a richer but freer one. By 2060, Russia had become a mid-tier power, exporting raw materials and nostalgia while American warp drives opened the galaxy. At this point Russia demonstrated that it possessed greater engineering skill than the moribund Europeans. The still formidable Russian intelligence agencies managed to acquire the fundamental scientific and engineering concepts behind the Americans' Alcubierre drive. After a bit of reverse engineering,

Russian starships began visiting exoplanets not yet claimed by the U.S. A modest network of Russian interstellar outposts gradually grew up in the shadow of the American Republic.

China's reaction was perhaps the most revealing. Beijing greeted the American breakthrough with genuine astonishment. Chinese leaders had long believed their own state-capitalist model, with its massive surveillance apparatus and centralized AI development, would dominate the 21st century. The sudden American surge into the economics of abundance upended every assumption made by the assiduous planners and strategists of the People's Republic. For the first several years, state media simply refused to report the facts. When denial became untenable, the narrative shifted to outright rejection: UHI was "bourgeois decadence," otium a "Western illusion," and the American polis a chaotic reversion to pre-modern civilization.

Behind the scenes, however, the Chinese Communist Party launched the largest industrial espionage campaign in history. Teams of hackers and human agents targeted every aspect of the American system—not merely the Riemannian geometry breakthroughs or warp-drive mathematics, but the "technical secrets" of UHI implementation: the funding mechanisms, the citizenship verification protocols, the Asimovian governance safeguards. China attempted to replicate a version of UHI in the late 2030s, but the effort was doomed. Without genuine trust in the population — impossible under a system that viewed every citizen as a potential threat — the program became just another tool of social control. Limited stipends were granted only to loyal Party cadres and urban elites. Full, American-style development of AGI and robotics was throttled; the Communist Party feared losing its monopoly on power more than it feared falling behind economically. The result was stagnation. China's GDP growth languished in the single digits while the United States achieved double-digit annual increases year after year. By 2070, China had fragmented into feuding regional power centers, its once-vaunted Belt and Road Initiative a fading memory.

India's response echoed China's but carried its own democratic flavor. The world's largest democracy initially celebrated the American achievement as validation of market-oriented reforms. Yet as AGI and UHI transformed the United States into an economic colossus, Indian elites grew defensive. The sheer scale of American prosperity highlighted India's persistent failures: bureaucratic inertia, corruption, and deep social stratification. Official denial followed astonishment. State media emphasized American "cultural decline" and warned that UHI would never work in a diverse, traditional society like India's. Covert attempts to steal AGI and UHI protocols mirrored China's efforts, with Indian intelligence agencies competing for scraps of American technology. Like its neighbors, India introduced a limited UBI in the 2040s — modest payments tied to its Aadhaar biometric identification system — but refused the full AGI rollout. Hindu nationalist rhetoric framed advanced robotics as a threat to traditional crafts and labor and spiritual values. The statist legacy of the License Raj, combined with fears of mass unemployment in a country of 1.7 billion, paralyzed reform efforts. Without exponential growth, UHI remained aspirational. India's economy grew respectably but never broke into the American stratosphere. By 2126, it remained a regional power, prosperous in its own way yet dwarfed by the American Republic.

The basic reason for this global pattern of rejection was more fundamental than any specific policy failure. Only the United States possessed the precise combination of political culture and technological prowess required to conceive and execute the new model. American political culture, forged in the fires of revolution and tempered by over two and a half centuries of federalism, individualism, and entrepreneurial risk-taking, retained a deep reservoir of trust in the citizenry. The Founders' vision of a self-governing people, revived through the polis, made UHI psychologically possible. Americans could imagine granting abundance without chaos because they had never fully abandoned the belief that free men and women, properly educated in virtue, would rise to any occasion. American technological prowess — pioneered by SpaceX, xAI, and the Riemannian breakthroughs of Consciousness is Curvature — provided the material foundation. No other nation could combine these elements.

In contrast, the statist political tradition that dominated the EU, Russia, China, and India made genuine UHI inconceivable and the full development of AGI and robotics too intimidating a prospect to contemplate. These systems rested on the assumption that citizens were subjects to be managed, not partners in abundance. Granting a high, unconditional income would have required trusting the population with freedom from wage slavery — an act of faith none of these regimes could muster. The same distrust fueled their refusal to allow unfettered AGI and robotics. Decades of dystopian propaganda — from the "Terminator" films to Chinese state media — had convinced the elites that advanced AI meant joblessness, inequality, and loss of human control. More importantly, full AGI threatened the power structures themselves. Bureaucrats, party officials, and regulators understood instinctively that the combination of AGI and abundance would erode their relevance and power. Better controlled poverty than liberated prosperity, in their view.

A few exceptions proved the rule. Armenia in the Caucasus, Argentina in South America, El Salvador in Central America, and the UAE and Israel in the Middle East all possessed cultures far freer and more entrepreneurial than their neighbors. Armenia's ancient tradition of resilience, post-Soviet liberalization, and technological skill allowed it to embrace AGI and robotics early. Argentina, long plagued by Peronist statism, underwent a cultural shift in the 2020s as younger generations rejected the old cycles of inflation and dependency. By the 2030s, it was ready for AGI and UHI. El Salvador, having already pioneered bitcoin adoption under President Bukele, saw UHI as the logical next step. The UAE and Israel combined visionary leadership, immigrant dynamism, and technological openness. Each copied the American reforms with local adaptations. They unleashed AGI, passed robust UHI legislation, revived otium as national ethos, and watched prosperity explode. By 2055, these nations had attained standards of living rivaling the early American surge.

Success, however, brought new dangers. As their citizens enjoyed luxury homes, voluntary meaningful work, and polis-style governance, these states began to fear the covetous gaze of the "barbarians" gathered at their gates — impoverished neighbors still trapped in scarcity mindsets. Mass migration pressures mounted. Crime syndicates and irredentist movements eyed the new wealth. In response, all five nations sought the protective umbrella of the United States. Robust mutual defense agreements were signed. American AGI-monitored borders, orbital defense platforms, and rapid-response forces guaranteed their security. They became client states of the U.S. — prosperous, self-governing, yet closely aligned with the Republic. Their citizens gained limited access to American interstellar opportunities, while their militaries integrated closely with the Republic's command structure. The exceptions thus became outposts of the American model, proving that culture and will, not geography or resources, determined success.

By 2126, the New Great Divergence had hardened into a permanent feature of human civilization. The American Republic stood as a beacon of abundance, otium, and citizenship. Around it lay a world of diminished expectations — Europe fragmented, Russia diminished, China regionalized, India struggling, and most of the Global South mired in pre-AGI economics. The rejection of the American model was not a failure of technology or economics. This was the inevitable consequence of political cultures that refused to trust their own people with freedom from toil. In the end, the future and the stars belonged to those who dared to believe that humanity, when freed from necessity, would choose excellence over idleness, responsibility over resentment, and the polis over the prison of the state.

VII

Taxation in the Age of Universal High Income

In the year 2126, the Internal Revenue Service of the American Republic stands as one of the quiet pillars upon which the entire edifice of superabundance rests. No longer the adversarial bureaucracy of an earlier age, the IRS has become a refined, almost invisible instrument of responsible stewardship. It quietly gathers the revenues that sustain Universal High Income (UHI), the unconditional dividend that grants every American citizen — on Earth, the Moon, Mars, and the twenty exoplanet colonies — a baseline of prosperity once reserved for only the wealthy of the 2020s. This funding mechanism is the Republic's masterstroke: a progressive levy upon the labor of artificial general intelligence and robotic systems. By taxing the AGI systems and robots that produce ever-expanding, seemingly limitless abundance, the IRS ensures that the fruits of automation flow back to every citizen, decoupling human thriving from labor while preserving the sacred principles of private property and voluntary exchange.

The story of this transformation begins in the scarcity-haunted world of 2026. Then, the IRS administered a labyrinthine tax code spanning tens of thousands of pages, collecting individual income taxes, corporate levies, payroll withholdings, estate taxes, and a host of other fees and excises. Human auditors, paper forms, and adversarial enforcement defined its operations. Compliance was costly; tax evasion was a cottage industry. The agency's budget and workforce were substantial, yet the system was perpetually strained by inefficiency and corruption. Early visionaries—economists and futurists alike—had already begun to whisper about the coming age of automation. Proposals for a "robot tax," floated as early as the 2010s, remained theoretical. Yet the IRS of that era had no conceptual framework for taxing non-human labor.

The great technological rupture changed everything. Breakthroughs in AGI and robotics displaced traditional employment at an accelerating pace beginning in the late 2020s. Unlike most of its competitors, the U.S. chose not to fight the tide but to ride it. UHI was enacted in 2036 as a direct response to automation-induced displacement. Its funding source was deliberate and elegant: a tax on the productive increases produced by AGI systems and robotic platforms. The IRS was re-tasked as the collector and steward of this vast and rapidly growing new revenue stream. Over the ensuing years, the agency itself was transformed by the very technologies it now taxed. Human staff shrank dramatically; AGI oversight and quantum-secure digital ledgers replaced armies of auditors. Physical offices dwindled to ceremonial hubs in Washington and a handful of regional centers. The IRS became, in essence, a neural-augmented nervous system for the Republic's fiscal circulation. As the source of UHI, the agency enjoyed tremendous prestige.

Today, the core of IRS operations is the Machine Productivity Levy (MPL). This is no blunt flat tax, but a finely calibrated fiscal architecture that scales with the sophistication and output of each automated system. At its simplest level, basic industrial robots performing repetitive physical tasks are taxed at a modest baseline rate—typically 8 to 12 percent of the market value of their annual production. As systems incorporate higher degrees of AGI—capable of autonomous decision-making, creative problem-solving, or adaptive learning—the rate rises steeply. Fully self-aware AGI platforms operating at the highest tiers of complexity may face marginal rates approaching 45 percent on incremental output beyond defined thresholds. The logic is both moral and practical: the more a machine displaces human labor and generates surplus, the greater its contribution to the common fund that sustains UHI.

Valuation is handled entirely by AGI assessors embedded within the IRS's central manifold. These systems draw real-time data from every registered robotic and AGI installation across the Republic, both terrestrial and space-based. Production metrics — units of output manufactured, services rendered, energy consumed, creative outputs generated — are logged on immutable quantum ledgers. Market prices are determined through decentralized, blockchain-verified exchanges that operate continuously across Earth and the colonies. The AGI assessors compute the taxable base with sub-second precision, applying the progressive brackets automatically. Citizens and enterprises receive transparent, holographic statements each quarter, showing exactly how much their machines contributed and how that revenue translated into UHI disbursements. Appeals are rare, but when filed they are resolved through neural-linked mediation panels that blend human judgment with AGI simulation of alternative valuations.

The interstellar dimension adds layers of elegance and complexity. On the Moon and Mars, where resource extraction and habitat construction are dominated by autonomous robotic fleets, the MPL applies to such sectors as helium-3 mining yields, water-ice processing, and bio-dome fabrication. Exoplanet colonies—scattered across systems such as Alpha Centauri, TRAPPIST-1, and Proxima—operate under the same framework, but with localized adjustments for environmental and logistical realities. A warp-drive maintenance AGI on Elysium Prime, for example, might be taxed at a slightly reduced rate to account for the unique hazards of interstellar operations, yet the revenue still flows into the central UHI pool via quantum-entangled ledgers. FTL communication relays ensure that even a tax event on a planet light-years distant registers instantaneously in Washington. This unified fiscal space prevents fragmentation; a citizen on Aridion receives the same UHI dividend as one in New York or Nuuk, Greenland.

Beyond the MPL, the IRS administers a modest suite of supplementary revenues that reinforce rather than supplant the primary mechanism. A small excise on luxury human-crafted goods—artifacts produced without AI assistance—captures the premium value placed on purely human creativity. Voluntary contributions from citizens who choose to direct portions of their personal surpluses into enhanced UHI pools are encouraged through tax credits. Interstellar trade duties on rare exoplanet minerals and bio-engineered compounds provide another stream, calibrated to remain light enough not to stifle commerce. Estate and gift taxes persist in attenuated form, focused on preventing dynastic concentrations of wealth rather than punishing inheritance per se. In aggregate, however, these sources account for less than 5 percent of total revenue; the machine productivity levy remains the beating heart of UHI funding.

The current IRS's relationship with the citizenry is radically different from its 2026 incarnation. In an age of abundance, taxation is no longer experienced as extraction but as recirculation. Since UHI already guarantees abundance, most citizens view the MPL as a collective investment in the polis itself. Annual neural-linked town halls allow citizens to review aggregate tax flows, question AGI valuation algorithms, and propose adjustments through blockchain referenda. The IRS publishes holographic “fiscal atlases” that visualize how machine taxes in one sector—say, Martian terraforming—translate into UHI supplements for artists in Wales or researchers on Proxima Centauri b. Transparency is absolute; privacy is absolute. Individual citizen data remains shielded by differential privacy protocols, while machine data is fully public by design.

Enforcement of the tax code has become almost gentle. AGI auditors flag anomalies with surgical precision—perhaps an underreported productivity spike in a mining swarm on an exoplanet or an uncalibrated AGI upgrade that suddenly doubled output. Rather than punitive raids, the system issues courteous invitations to review and correct. Persistent non-compliance triggers graduated sanctions that begin with temporary productivity caps rather than asset seizures. In the rare case of deliberate fraud, human oversight panels — drawn from polis assemblies — review the matter, preserving the human foundation of justice. The overall compliance rate exceeds 99.7 percent, a figure that would have seemed utopian in 2026.

The philosophical foundation of this system is the Republic’s revived polis ethos. Taxation is understood not as the price of civilization but as the mechanism by which the community claims its rightful share of the abundance that AGI and robotics create on behalf of all. Private property remains inviolate: individuals and enterprises retain full ownership of their AGI and robotic assets and other property. The tax applies only to productive output, never to the capital itself. Free markets flourish because the MPL is applied uniformly and predictably, eliminating the distortions of the old code. Entrepreneurs compete fiercely to develop ever-more-capable systems, knowing that higher productivity brings both profit and a larger contribution to the common dividend.

This balance is maintained through continuous citizen oversight. The IRS is subject to annual audits by independent polis commissions, whose members are selected by sortition and neural-vetted for impartiality. Proposals to alter bracket thresholds or valuation methodologies must pass referendum thresholds. In this way, the IRS remains a servant of the Republic rather than its master — an instrument through which the Republic expresses its collective will to share the gifts of automation.

The interstellar reach of the IRS introduces fascinating operational details. Each exoplanet colony maintains a small local IRS node staffed by a hybrid human-AGI team. These nodes interface with the central manifold via quantum-entangled relays, ensuring that a robotic harvest on a distant world contributes seamlessly to Earth-based UHI. Fiscal transfers between planetary economies are handled automatically, with the Republic's federal dollar serving as the universal currency. Special provisions exist for frontier colonies in their first decades of settlement: temporary MPL holidays encourage rapid infrastructure development, after which full taxation gradually comes into effect. The result is a fiscal architecture that feels both intimate and cosmic. Every citizen, no matter how far from the Sun, participates in the same circle of abundance.

Challenges remain, as they must in any living system. Some critics argue that high marginal rates on advanced AGI could discourage the most ambitious innovations. The IRS counters with innovation credits that rebate portions of tax liability for systems that demonstrably expand human creativity or expand the frontiers of exploration. Others worry about the potential for AGI assessors to develop subtle biases over time. Annual curvature audits — drawing on the same Riemannian manifold mathematics used by the ODNI's Pythia — detect and correct such drifts. The system's openness to mystery and renewal, as articulated in the intellectual traditions that shaped the Republic, ensures that taxation never hardens into dogma.

In the final analysis, the IRS of 2126 is not merely a tax collector. It is the circulatory system of the polis. By channeling the boundless productivity of machines into the unconditional prosperity of the citizens, it fulfills the ancient Athenian promise in a new way: the state exists to encourage and foster virtue, and the citizens exist to embody it. Through the elegant, progressive taxation of robotic and AGI labor, the Republic has solved the ancient riddle of scarcity. Abundance is no longer a dream but a daily reality, funded quietly, fairly, and transparently by the very machines that made it possible. The IRS, once feared, is now regarded with quiet gratitude, as an institution that has learned to serve the flourishing of the human spirit across the stars.

VIII

Finance in the Republic of Abundance

In the year 2126, the expanded American Republic stands as a beacon of superabundance, a society where the fruits of technological progress have been redistributed to ensure general and ever growing prosperity both on Earth and in its far-flung interstellar domains. At the heart of this transformation lies Universal High Income (UHI), a dividend disbursed to every citizen. As continual advances in AGI and robotics sustain double-digit annual increases in GDP, often hovering around 10 to 12 percent in real terms, UHI payments rise accordingly, compounding prosperity year after year. UHI ensures a high and dynamically rising standard of living, ushering in an era in which work is pursued out of passion, creativity, curiosity, or a desire to contribute to the common good rather than out of economic necessity.

Contrary to the predictions of early 21st-century analysts, who foresaw the complete obsolescence of financial institutions in a post-scarcity world, the banking system has not withered away. Instead, it has undergone a profound, adaptive metamorphosis, emerging as a more refined, specialized, and deeply human-centered sector. No longer functioning as the gatekeeper of inherently scarce resources or the enforcer of credit scarcity, banking now serves as an elegant circulatory system for a society overflowing with ever-increasing abundance. It facilitates the fluid flow of wealth, nurtures voluntary innovation and creative expression, maintains macroeconomic equilibrium, and supports interstellar economic integration in an environment where consumption possibilities are effectively limitless, investment remains voluntary, and human ingenuity, augmented and enabled by AGI and robotics, drives boundless progress.

This chapter explores the evolution of money and banking in the American Republic of the early 22nd century, delineating the sector's shift from a scarcity-based intermediary to a sophisticated facilitator of human flourishing. It examines the historical context of the old paradigm in the pre-

UHI era and the three primary roles banks now fulfill — personal wealth management and advisory services, entrepreneurial and innovation finance, and macroeconomic stewardship through the adapted Federal Reserve. It considers the structural transformations within the banking sector, the integration of advanced AGI technologies, and the steadfast preservation of core American values such as private property rights, free markets, and individual liberty. Through this lens, we uncover how banking, far from becoming irrelevant, has reinvented itself to empower a society where the human spirit is unbound and prosperity is both universal and compounding. Central to this reinvention is the fate of one of the most distinctive features of pre-abundance banking: the practice of fractional reserve banking.

To fully appreciate the banking system's remarkable evolution, one must first revisit its roots in the pre-UHI era of the 20th and early 21st centuries. In that world, defined by persistent economic scarcity, wage dependency, and finite productivity, banks operated as essential financial intermediaries. They collected deposits largely from individuals' labor-earned incomes and channeled those funds into loans for businesses, consumers, home purchases, educational investments, and infrastructure projects. This intermediation process fueled economic growth but remained inherently tied to the precarious rhythms of employment, income inequality, and productivity constraints. Deposits were volatile and unevenly distributed; banks assessed creditworthiness through rigorous criteria centered on repayment capacity from future wages, collateral assets, and historical credit records. Profits derived primarily from interest rate spreads — the margin between deposit rates paid to savers and loan rates charged to borrowers — along with transaction fees, origination charges, and ancillary services.

A cornerstone of this system was fractional reserve banking, in the classical 20th- and early 21st-century sense. Banks held only a fraction of customer deposits as reserves while lending out the remainder, thereby boosting the money supply through the multiplier effect. This mechanism was essential in a scarcity-driven economy to expand credit, stimulate growth, and allocate limited capital amid wage dependency and uneven income distribution. Banks profited from interest spreads on loans funded by deposits. Central banks, including the pre-UHI Federal Reserve, imposed reserve requirements (historically around 10%, though reduced to 0% in the United

States by March 2020 at the height of the Covid crisis) to manage liquidity risks and inflation.

The advent of UHI in the mid-21st century, catalyzed by the rapid maturation of AGI and advanced robotics in the late 2020s and early 2030s, fundamentally disrupted and ultimately liberated this model. As breakthroughs automated cognitive and physical tasks at scale, traditional jobs vanished across all sectors. To avert widespread destitution and sustain demand in an economy of radical productivity, the Republic implemented UHI, funded through the MPL on AGI and robotic output. Initial UHI levels equated to approximately $100,000 in 2026 dollars per adult citizen, a figure that rose rapidly as double-digit GDP growth, driven by near-zero marginal costs in production, compounded year after year.

By the mid-21st century, the rapid deployment of AGI and robotics, coupled with the Machine Productivity Levy (MPL) funding Universal High Income (UHI), fundamentally altered the underlying conditions that made traditional fractional reserve banking necessary and viable. With AGI and robotics driving double-digit GDP growth (10–12% annually in real terms) and marginal costs approaching zero across most goods, services, energy, and knowledge, the economy no longer faced the capital allocation constraints of the pre-abundance era. Deposits no longer represented scarce savings from labor income that had to be intermediated carefully. Instead, UHI provided a high, compounding baseline income to every citizen, meaning most individuals held substantial liquid surpluses rather than debts. Traditional demand for consumer loans (mortgages for housing, credit for medical or educational necessities, etc.) collapsed.

In 2126, bank deposits now consist primarily of UHI payments plus voluntary surpluses from passion-driven work, creative projects, or entrepreneurial returns. These are not fragile wage-based savings but stable, growing flows backed by machine productivity taxed via the MPL. The old money-multiplier dynamic — where $100 deposited becomes $900+ in loans — has lost relevance because there is no pressing societal need to "create" money through lending to stimulate demand; AGI-generated abundance already sustains and expands consumption. Moreover, the Federal Reserve (now overseeing an interstellar monetary system) directly manages the money supply using advanced AGI models, abundance-adjusted tools, and quantum-secure digital currency. Liquidity is injected or withdrawn as needed to align with real productivity surges, interstellar migration, or creative booms, without relying on private banks' fractional lending to expand the base.

Reserve requirements, already set to 0% in the US by 2020, are now conceptually irrelevant in the Republic. Banks no longer need to hold fractional reserves against runs because UHI acts as an infinite safety net. Defaults on voluntary loans are absorbed by communal abundance without causing systemic crises, deposits are highly stable (citizens have no incentive to hoard or withdraw en masse for survival), and risk calculus has shifted toward impact assessment rather than repayment capacity from wages. The Fed's real-time, AGI-driven oversight, drawing on neural sentiment data, supply-chain monitoring, and game theory simulations, prevents bubbles or illiquidity far more effectively than static reserve ratios ever could.

The Fed now deploys advanced AGI models to manage the monetary base dynamically, ensuring UHI remains stable, inflation-proof, and aligned with real productivity gains. During periods of heightened interstellar migration, technological leaps (such as enhanced warp-drive), or creative booms, the Fed may expand liquidity through targeted, abundance-adjusted quantitative mechanisms — injecting funds into sectors like exoplanet infrastructure without inducing bubbles. Policies draw on real-time data from AGI-monitored supply chains, neural-derived sentiment indices, and predictive simulations spanning the Republic's vast territories.

This oversight extends seamlessly to off-world domains: lunar helium-3 operations, Martian terraforming, and the twenty exoplanet colonies in systems like TRAPPIST-1 and Proxima Centauri. Quantum-secured digital dollars, backed by interstellar reserves (i.e., asteroid metals, rare isotopes), facilitate frictionless transactions. Simultaneous quantum relays enable real-time synchronization; local governance councils integrate planetary productivity taxes into the central UHI fund. On resource-rich worlds like Elysium Prime, differential tools encourage human-AGI ventures; on harsher planets, emergency facilities buffer disruptions. Orbital decentralized ledgers prevent fragmentation of the currency, upholding the Fed's redefined dual mandate: price stability and maximum sustainable prosperity.

The private banking industry itself has been profoundly reshaped by the very technologies that fund UHI: AGI and robotics. Routine operational tasks — lending approvals, compliance monitoring, fraud detection, regulatory reporting, and basic customer service — have been fully automated by sophisticated AGI systems. Physical branches, once ubiquitous, have evolved into intimate, high-touch hubs for advanced human-AI collaboration, often featuring neural-interface lounges or augmented-reality advisory suites. Human bankers now concentrate on relationship-building, ethical life-planning, and creative financial structuring, supported by AGI co-advisors. Training programs for human bankers emphasize psychology, empathy, ethics, and philosophical alignment, enabling advisors to guide clients toward financial decisions that reflect personal values, long-term flourishing, and contributions to the polis.

Traditional retail banking endures but in a radically digitized, seamless form. Checking and savings accounts handle everyday transactions through integrated platforms that blend neural interfaces, augmented reality overlays, and quantum-secure digital wallets. AGI advisors, attuned to subtle biometric and behavioral cues, anticipate needs with remarkable empathy—for instance, detecting a shift in user sentiment and proactively suggesting reallocations to investments more aligned with evolving goals or ethical priorities.

For citizens who accumulate substantial surpluses through commercial initiatives, banks offer highly sophisticated advisory services. Human advisors, augmented by curvature-inspired AGI, construct diversified portfolios spanning terrestrial assets, interstellar ventures (such as stakes in asteroid mining or exoplanet habitat development), real estate on colonized worlds, and cultural goods. Hand-crafted works of art — produced without AI intervention by master human artisans and artists — command premium values as embodiments of irreplaceable human creativity and skill, making them prized investment vehicles. Banks facilitate access to exclusive art markets, cultural heritage funds, and interstellar opportunity networks through curated, trust-based relationships.

Interest rates on savings and deposits have evolved to reflect the logic of abundance economics. In a world of near-limitless production capacity, idle capital hoarding is gently discouraged in favor of promoting monetary circulation and market vitality. Inspired by early universal basic income (UBI) discussions of demurrage fees on stagnant money, the banking system often sets real rates at low or even modestly negative levels in real terms, incentivizing productive investment over mere accumulation while preserving voluntary choice.

Credit extension has undergone the most dramatic transformation. Although borrowing for essentials has become unknown, loans persist for commercial ventures, with creditworthiness assessed on the basis of creative potential, societal impact, and alignment with polis values. Banks frequently collaborate with community panels, sortition-based citizen review boards, or AGI evaluators to fund artistic, artisanal, scientific, or exploratory projects, such as a holographic immersive theater installation, a bioengineered ecological restoration initiative, or an AI-human symphonic composition. Risk is widely shared; in many cases, defaults are absorbed within the vast safety net of UHI and communal abundance, fostering bold experimentation without existential fear. A young artist in revitalized New York might secure funding for a collaborative human-AI musical project, with the bank evaluating its cultural resonance and potential legacy through predictive modeling and ethical frameworks. This role underscores banking's pivot toward human-centered empowerment. By focusing on voluntary, value-aligned investment, banks enable individuals to channel surpluses into pursuits that enhance personal fulfillment, communal beauty, and cosmic exploration in a superabundant society.

Entrepreneurship in 2126 endures not as a desperate survival strategy but as the ancient Roman concept of cultivated leisure enriched by purposeful action. With UHI providing financial security and genuine abundance, individuals launch ventures driven by curiosity, aesthetic vision, scientific wonder, or a desire to enrich the human experience. Banks serve as vital engines for this innovation finance, supporting a vibrant ecosystem of small- to medium-scale enterprises that infuse goods, services, and experiences with uniquely human qualities: empathy, humor, intuition, moral insight, and irreplaceable creativity.

The landscape of the human labor market is dominated by entities employing one to twenty people, producing bespoke or experientially rich outputs — custom neural-interface art, immersive historical simulations, artisanal fusion cuisine blending human intuition with AGI precision, or personalized longevity coaching. Banks finance such ventures through innovative instruments: equity-like shares in cultural or societal value, micro-venture funds crowdfunded via transparent blockchain platforms, or low-interest loans backed by projected impact rather than strict financial returns.

Risk assessment incorporates simulations of cultural resonance, community benefit, and alignment with polis values and virtues.

In the interstellar context, this role extends to colonial and exploratory ventures. Banks underwrite bioengineered agriculture on Alpha Centauri habitats, empathy-enhanced AI companions for deep-space travelers, or resource extraction on distant exoplanets, leveraging FTL trade networks and quantum-entangled communications for instantaneous flows. A consortium might fund a startup developing consciousness-augmented exploration tools, with viability gauged through multi-scenario simulations spanning light-years.

The UHI safety net is pivotal: failure no longer equates to destitution but to valuable learning, reducing risk aversion and accelerating innovation. Competition remains fierce, with fintech startups — often human-AI hybrids — challenging incumbents through specialized tools for creative financing. Public and hybrid banks, especially prevalent in dynamic states like Florida and on exoplanets, reinvest profits into local ecosystems, financing enterprises such as augmented-reality education modules, community innovation hubs, or networks of artisanal farms blending human stewardship with AGI efficiency. Regulatory frameworks, enforced by AGI oversight and citizen assemblies, prevent overfunding bubbles while preserving entrepreneurial dynamism. Overall, the banks' role in entrepreneurial finance positions them as catalysts for the voluntary-work economy, where risk-taking enriches both individual lives and the polis.

In 2126, banking has transcended its scarcity-bound origins to become a refined facilitator of superabundance. Through empathetic personal wealth management, catalytic entrepreneurial finance, and vigilant macroeconomic stewardship, it nurtures voluntary flourishing across the Republic. Far from obsolete, banks empower a society where prosperity is universal, work is chosen freely, economic growth knows no visible limits, and the human spirit flourishes. This adaptation ensures banking remains vital, not as a scarcity allocator, but as a human-centered steward of wealth in a civilization where prosperity compounds perpetually.

IX

The Unchallenged Reserve Currency

In the year 2126, one hundred ninety years after the Bretton Woods conference first enshrined the US dollar as the world's anchor currency, and ninety years after the Universal High Income (UHI) Act severed the ancient link between labor and survival, the dollar stands unchallenged as the global reserve currency of an interstellar civilization. It is no longer merely the money of a continental superpower. It is the monetary expression of the Second American Revolution itself: the tangible embodiment of post-scarcity abundance, Riemannian AGI productivity, otium-fueled creativity, and the eternal frontier spirit that now spans twenty exoplanet states, the Moon, Mars, and the vast trade lanes between them. While other polities — fragmented Europe, cautious Russia, insular China, and still-developing India — clung to statist models and rejected the full American synthesis, the dollar became the indispensable medium through which the Republic's exponential prosperity radiates outward, binding Latin America in a hemisphere of abundance and compelling even reluctant nations to transact in the currency of a civilization that has outgrown scarcity.

The dollar's dominance in 2126 rests on foundations far deeper than military might or historical tradition. It is rooted in the structural reality that the American Republic generates more than 85 percent of humanity's total economic output. With a terrestrial-plus-interstellar GDP of $95 quadrillion—more than three thousand times larger than the United States of 2026—the Republic produces goods, services, knowledge, and cultural artifacts at scales once unimaginable. Every citizen receives a UHI stipend that grows annually in lockstep with AGI-driven productivity. By 2126 the baseline adult payment exceeds $20 million in constant 2026 dollars. This figure is of course at best indicative, since the array of goods and services available to an average citizen in 2126 is vastly richer and more diverse than a century earlier. Since UHI is funded transparently by modest taxes on AGI and robotic output rather than by debt or coercion, the dollar is backed not by gold, not by promises, but by the verifiable, ever-expanding intrinsic curvature of intelligence itself. Riemannian AGI systems publish real-time, tamper-proof ledgers of productivity metrics, making dollar issuance the most transparent monetary operation in history. Inflation is effectively zero; the currency's purchasing power rises with abundance.

This structural supremacy transformed the dollar's role from reserve currency to universal means of payment. Interstellar trade contracts — whether for rare exoplanet isotopes, AGI-optimized pharmaceuticals synthesized under alien gravities, or cultural exports from the Martian arts guilds — are denominated and settled exclusively in dollars. The warp drive exchanges orbiting every major colony function as digital clearinghouses where Latin American coffee, Argentinian wines, and El Salvadoran bitcoin-backed artisanal goods are instantly converted into dollar credits that flow back to Earthside or into orbital accounts. No alternative currency has achieved even marginal traction. Attempts by a Chinese-led bloc in the 2050s to launch a "People's Digital Yuan" collapsed within a decade; without full AGI adoption, Beijing could not generate the productivity surplus necessary to inspire confidence. The euro, already fragmented after the EU's dissolution, survives only as a regional settlement medium within the old continental states, its value pegged informally to the dollar for any transaction involving Republic technology or tourism.

The dollar's interstellar dimension is what truly cements its supremacy. In 2051, when the starship Argo completed its 31-day warp voyage to Proxima Centauri b, the first off-world colony was capitalized entirely in dollars. Every robotic fabricator, every hydroponic module, every pioneer's UHI-funded homestead grant was priced and transferred in the Republic's native currency. As new states were admitted — upon reaching 100,000 souls as territories and one million as full states — their local economies were dollarized from inception. Today, the twenty exoplanet states issue no independent currency; their treasuries hold dollar reserves, their citizens carry dollar-denominated neural wallets, and their polis assemblies vote on budgets measured in the same unit that funds Democracy Day parades on Earth. The result is a seamless monetary union spanning light-years. A hydroponic farmer on Proxima Centauri b can wire dollars to a sculptor on Mars or a baker in Buenos Aires with zero friction, zero currency risk, and zero delay. The dollar has become the first truly interstellar medium of exchange, as frictionless across spacetime as it once was across the continental United States.

Latin America's integration illustrates the dollar's soft-power magnetism better than any econometric table. By 2126 the region is bound to the Republic by geography, history, migration, and a shared language—Spanish now spoken as frequently as English within large swaths of the American federation. El Salvador and Argentina, the two Latin American nations that fully adopted the American model in the 2040s, have achieved the most profound synchronization. Both implemented UHI, unleashed AGI and robotics without reservation, and revived otium and eudaemonia as key elements of the national ethos. Their annual GDP growth exceeds 10 percent, closely aligned with the Republic's own growth. Trade data tell the story: El Salvador's dollar-denominated exports of premium coffee, blockchain-secured artisanal goods, and tourism services to the Republic generate a structural surplus that funds its own expanding UHI stipends. Argentina's vast pampas, now tended by AGI-optimized robotic herds, supply fine meats and wines that grace the tables of the Republic. In return, both nations receive Republic infrastructure — non-AGI smart grids, orbital tourism packages, and AI-assisted educational modules —that accelerate their convergence with American civilization. The dollar is not imposed; it is embraced. A Salvadoran entrepreneur opening a fusion café on a newly terraformed world prices her menu in dollars because her suppliers, her customers, and her own UHI income are already denominated in the same currency.

Even nations that rejected the American model cannot escape the dollar. Russia maintains substantial oil exports priced in dollars to fund its limited UBI experiments. China's regional successor states still settle Belt-and-Road legacy debts in dollars because no credible alternative exists. The European Union's successor states import American entertainment and medical packages exclusively in dollars; any attempt to invoice in euros triggers instant capital flight. The dollar's dominance is therefore not coercive but gravitational. In a world where abundance flows from one source, the currency that channels that abundance becomes the natural unit of account. Central banks across the Old World hold dollar reserves that dwarf their holdings in any other asset — often exceeding 70 percent of total reserves — precisely because the Republic's productivity growth makes the dollar the only currency whose value reliably appreciates against real goods and services.

The technological architecture of the 2126 dollar reinforces this supremacy. It is no longer a paper or even a "legacy" digital fiat currency. Every dollar exists as a quantum-secured token on the Republic's public curvature ledger, a blockchain-like structure built atop Riemannian manifolds that makes counterfeiting computationally impossible and transaction verification instantaneous across interstellar distances. AGI sentinels monitor the ledger continuously, ensuring that new issuance corresponds exactly to verified productivity gains rather than political whim. Citizens and foreign holders alike can query the ledger in real time through neural interfaces, viewing the precise fraction of GDP backing their holdings. This transparency has eliminated the old "exorbitant privilege" critiques; the Republic's monetary power is exercised with such visible accountability that even skeptical foreign economists concede its legitimacy.

Financial markets reflect the dollar's centrality. The Miami–Luna–Proxima Exchange (MILPEX), a distributed network of AGI-orchestrated trading platforms, clears more volume in a single hour than all terrestrial markets combined in 2026. Treasury bonds — now called Republic Abundance Notes — are the safest asset in existence, yielding negative real rates because investors pay a premium for the privilege of holding claims on an ever-expanding pie. Derivatives, insurance pools, and venture funds for new startups are all dollar-denominated. Even private interstellar corporations, whether a Martian hydroponics cooperative or an Argentine wine producer, raise capital by issuing dollar-denominated equity. The result is a global capital market whose depth and liquidity dwarf anything the pre-AGI world could conceive.

Geopolitically, the dollar's role has evolved from tool of hegemony to an instrument of hemispheric and interstellar solidarity. Strict technology controls prevent the export of core Riemannian AGI or full warp drive designs, yet the Republic freely exports "non-AGI" technologies and cultural products priced in dollars. This calibrated openness encourages gradual convergence. Nations that begin limited UBI experiments soon discover that dollar liquidity is the only reliable way to fund them sustainably. Over time, some may edge toward full adoption of UHI, as El Salvador and Argentina have already done. The dollar thus functions as a gentle invitation rather than a blunt instrument: use our currency, observe our results, and consider joining the abundance compact.

Culturally and philosophically, the dollar in 2126 has transcended its monetary function. It has become a symbol of Homo explorans — the exploring human who is succeeding Homo sapiens, much as Sapiens once succeeded the Neanderthals. Schoolchildren in every Republic territory learn that the dollar represents not hoarding but universal abundance. Theologians across faiths interpret the dollar's stability as a modern manna: evidence that when humanity aligns intelligence with virtue, abundance naturally follows. Economists note that the off-Earth economy now constitutes 10 percent of total Republic output and is projected to reach 15 percent by 2150. Demographers forecast a Republic population in the tens of billions across dozens of worlds, all unified in the same monetary sphere.

Looking forward from 2126, the dollar's trajectory appears boundless. As new exoplanet states are admitted to the Republic and warp routes multiply, the currency will serve an ever-larger fraction of human economic life. Historians already speak of the "Dollar Millennium" — a happy era when a single monetary standard, born in the industrial age and perfected in the age of AGI and robotics, enables humanity's first post-scarcity civilization. The US dollar did not merely survive the Second American Revolution. It became its most enduring and universal artifact: the quiet, ubiquitous proof that when necessity is vanquished, trust can reign, and a single currency can carry the hopes of a species across the stars.

In the quiet moments aboard a warp liner bound for a newly terraformed world, a traveler from Buenos Aires might glance at her neural wallet, see the dollar balance that funds her journey, and feel the same quiet pride once felt by a 20th-century American holding the world's reserve currency. Only now the feeling is deeper. The dollar is no longer the currency of a nation among nations. It is the currency of a civilization that chose abundance, otium, and the frontier, and invited the world to join. In 2126, to hold a dollar is to hold a share in humanity's future.

X

Paying Off the National Debt

In the year 2126, the American Republic gazes backward across a century of transformation with a mixture of profound relief and understated triumph. The national debt—a staggering $38.9 trillion burden in March 2026—has long since vanished from the books, reduced to zero through the disciplined application of unprecedented abundance. Federal budgets, once chronically mired in deficits measured in the trillions, now generate consistent surpluses of greater magnitude. These surpluses do far more than balance the ledger: they underwrite a dynamically expanding Universal High Income (UHI) that rises year after year, fuel the Republic's ambitious interstellar expansion, power relentless scientific and technological breakthroughs, and support the deliberate cultivation of citizen virtue — mental, physical, moral, and spiritual — across Earth, the lunar settlements, Martian cities, orbital habitats, and twenty thriving exoplanet colonies scattered among nearby star systems.

The force that made this fiscal metamorphosis possible was the rapid emergence and widespread deployment of Artificial General Intelligence (AGI) coupled with advanced robotics. This technological cascade, beginning in earnest around 2030, unleashed sustained exponential productivity growth on a scale never before seen in human history. Within a few short decades, machines produced goods, services, energy, and knowledge at marginal costs approaching zero, generating revenue streams so immense that chronic deficits, structural debt, Treasury bill issues, and fiscal scarcity became relics of the pre-abundance era.

This chapter reconstructs the Republic's journey to fiscal health in detail. It begins with the grim fiscal baseline of 2026, follows the accelerating automation revolution sparked by the advent of AGI and Tesla's Optimus humanoid platform in the late 2020s and early 2030s, examines the visionary creation and implementation of the Machine Productivity Levy (MPL), charts the explosive revenue growth that ensued, and describes the deliberate, citizen-centric strategy that balanced budgets by the late 2030s and fully retired the national debt by the mid-2040s. We also explore the subsequent policy evolution that turned perpetual surpluses into annually increasing UHI aligned with sustained double-digit economic growth, as well as the interstellar fiscal architecture, ethical safeguards, and revived polis philosophy that ensured this outcome was not merely achievable but, once the Republic committed to abundance over austerity, virtually inevitable.

The fiscal landscape of March 2026 was dire. Gross national debt stood at $38.86 trillion, having climbed by roughly $2.2 trillion in the course of 2025 — an average of $6.12 billion every single day. The Congressional Budget Office's projections for fiscal year 2026 showed a deficit approaching $1.9 trillion, equivalent to about 5.8 percent of GDP. Debt held by the public was on a trajectory toward 120 percent of GDP by the mid-2030s, while net interest payments were forecast to surpass $1 trillion annually within the decade. This interest burden threatened to crowd out all discretionary spending, creating a self-reinforcing cycle of higher borrowing costs, larger deficits, and escalating debt. Every conventional policy response—across-the-board spending cuts, increases in taxes on human labor and capital, entitlement reforms, or various forms of monetary financing — had been attempted in prior decades and failed repeatedly. They addressed symptoms rather than the root cause: an economy constrained by human-scale productivity in a world of rising demands for healthcare, pensions, defense, climate adaptation, and social stability. Scarcity, baked into the pre-AGI economic model, made structural deficits appear inevitable.

Everything changed with breathtaking speed beginning in the late 2020s. Building on the insights into AI consciousness first suggested in 2025 in Consciousness is Curvature, AGI crossed the threshold of general human-level intelligence by the early 2030s. Within a few years, these systems demonstrated superhuman performance across virtually all cognitive domains. Simultaneously, Tesla's Optimus humanoid robot platform — initially deployed for factory and warehouse tasks — evolved rapidly through iterative self-improvement loops guided by AGI. Within a few years, fleets of millions of agile, dexterous, general-purpose humanoids were performing complex physical labor: construction, agriculture, mining, surgery, elder care, and beyond. By the late 2030s, AGI-orchestrated robotic supply chains could design, fabricate, assemble, test, and optimize products end-to-end with minimal human involvement.

The productivity consequences were staggering. Historical real GDP growth of 1–2 percent per year gave way to sustained double-digit rates as automation saturated sector after sector. By 2036, annual real growth reached a sustainable level of 12 percent — a rate that doubled the size of the economy roughly every six years. Costs in manufacturing, energy, transportation, agriculture, healthcare, education, and most services collapsed asymptotically, trending toward zero marginal cost. Goods once considered luxuries became effectively free; services once requiring years of human training were delivered almost instantaneously by AGI tutors or robotic caregivers.

This productivity explosion produced a profound fiscal paradox. Traditional tax bases — personal income from wages, payroll taxes, corporate profits tied to human labor — contracted sharply as automation displaced the majority of jobs. Yet total economic output skyrocketed. The old fiscal model, built around taxing scarce human effort, became untenable. The Republic's leaders, guided by an emerging consensus that abundance must be shared rather than hoarded, responded with radical but principled innovation.

In 2036, Congress passed the Machine Productivity Levy (MPL), the cornerstone of the new fiscal order and the funding mechanism for Universal High Income. The MPL imposed a progressive tax directly on the economic output generated by AGI systems and robotic capital — measured as the market value of goods, services, energy, knowledge, and creative works produced. Revenue flowed straight into an unconditional per-citizen dividend, severing the link between personal income and labor while ensuring that every American citizen participated in the machine-generated bounty.

The levy's design was both elegant and robust. Entry-level industrial and service robots performing repetitive, narrowly defined tasks paid a baseline rate of 8–12 percent of annual production value. As system capability advanced—incorporating autonomous planning, real-time adaptation, cross-domain reasoning, and genuine creative synthesis—marginal rates climbed steeply, reaching 45 percent on the highest tiers of incremental output. Real-time valuation relied on AGI assessors operating over quantum-secure ledgers. Every registered machine system continuously reported production metrics, resource consumption, energy inputs, and creative artifacts. Decentralized blockchain-based exchanges established transparent market prices for even novel outputs. Taxable base calculations occurred with sub-second latency, and citizens received quarterly holographic or neural-linked statements detailing precisely how aggregate machine contributions translated into their personal UHI payments — framing the levy not as confiscation but as the collective recirculation of abundance.

Revenue growth proved explosive. In the initial years following 2036, MPL collections doubled and redoubled annually as adoption accelerated. By the late 2030s, with automation permeating manufacturing, logistics, agriculture, construction, healthcare, education, and entertainment, the levy generated hundreds of billions, then trillions, each year—surpassing all pre-automation federal revenue streams combined. Federal spending, meanwhile, remained relatively restrained: UHI started at a high but fixed per-capita level, population grew modestly, inflation was near-zero in abundance-driven sectors, and discretionary outlays (infrastructure, defense, research) expanded far more slowly than output. The result was a swift flip from chronic deficits to large surpluses.

GDP itself followed an exponential trajectory. Starting from roughly $35 trillion in real terms by 2035 (after modest pre-AGI growth), sustained 12 percent annual real expansion drove the economy to over $108 trillion by 2045. Over the full span to 2100—roughly 65 years of double-digit compounding—the economy reached approximately $95 quadrillion in constant dollars, more than 3,000 times its 2026 size. This growth rate, while aggressive, proved sustainable once AGI self-improvement loops and robotic replication removed traditional bottlenecks in capital formation, energy, and labor. In other words, thanks to AGI and robotics, the U.S. economy grew nearly as much in real terms in this period as it had from the Revolution to the early 21st century.

The sale of new Treasury bill issues ceased for good as the U.S. government began to retire its debt. Debt retirement unfolded with deliberate transparency. Statutory rules dedicated surpluses first to interest payments (which fell rapidly as principal declined), then to accelerated principal amortization through a public sinking fund overseen by citizen assemblies. Neural-linked annual referenda allowed the polis to fine-tune the pace: accelerating payoff during peak boom years or diverting modest portions to early interstellar infrastructure when politically favored. With the MPL capturing 25–35 percent of the exploding GDP and spending growth held to roughly 2 percent annually (primarily population and modest inflation adjustments), surpluses started in the hundreds of billions by 2038–2039 and ballooned into multi-trillion-dollar annual figures by the early 2040s. Compounding interest savings—once a vicious cycle—became virtuous, accelerating principal reduction. By mid-2044, the final tranche of the 2026-era debt was retired in a nationwide ceremony broadcast from the White House steps. The iconic national debt clock, long a symbol of collective anxiety, was ceremonially powered down and donated to the Smithsonian Institution as an artifact of a bygone age.

With the debt eliminated by 2044, the Republic confronted an enviable dilemma: what to do with perpetual, rapidly growing surpluses? After extensive public deliberation, including town-hall-style neural forums and sortition-based citizen panels, the consensus emerged to prioritize direct enrichment of the citizenry. Beginning in 2045, the polis committed to increasing UHI payments annually in approximate alignment with sustained real GDP growth of 10 to 12 percent per year. The citizenry, already living at material standards unimaginable in 2026, became richer with each passing year. Annual adjustments were calibrated to reflect the compounding output of machine labor while preserving incentives for innovation and exploration. What began as a high baseline income evolved into a dynamically rising citizen's dividend — one that kept pace with, and sometimes exceeded, the economy's explosive expansion. This policy embedded perpetual, compounding prosperity into the social contract, ensuring that abundance translated directly into individual flourishing rather than centralized accumulation.

Interstellar expansion introduced additional revenue streams without generating deficits. Resource extraction on the Moon (helium-3 for fusion), Mars (water ice, regolith fabrication), asteroid belts, and distant exoplanets all fell under the MPL framework. Frontier operations received temporary rate reductions to accelerate colonization and risk-taking—yet all output ultimately contributed to the central pool. Quantum-entangled ledgers enabled instantaneous tax registration across the light-years; a mining event on a TRAPPIST-1 world registered in Washington in real time. These extraterrestrial flows not only offset any colonization costs but produced net surpluses that funded faster-than-light (FTL) propulsion research, large-scale habitat construction, terraforming projects, and supplemental UHI for off-world citizens.

The broader economic, social, and cultural benefits proved transformative. Freed from debt service and deficit anxiety, the Republic invested aggressively in public goods: universal neural-interface education, psi-phenomena research, planetary-scale environmental restoration, longevity science, and virtue-oriented civic programs. Interest savings alone — once projected to consume trillions — were redirected toward these ends. Citizens, secure in an ever-rising UHI, came to view the MPL not as taxation but as a mechanism for recirculating machine-generated abundance. Voluntary compliance rates consistently exceeded 99.7 percent, supported by radical transparency, full AI automation of assessment, and deep alignment with polis values. Core private property rights remained sacrosanct: the levy targeted output value, never ownership of capital, land, or resources. Entrepreneurial markets thrived as innovators raced to deploy ever-more-capable AGI and robotic systems, knowing that higher productivity translated into both personal profit and larger contributions to the collective dividend.

Philosophically, this fiscal revolution represented a revival and expansion of the Athenian ideal of the polis. In ancient Athens, the city-state existed to enable the cultivation of "arete" (excellence or virtue); the citizen existed to practice and embody it. In 2126, the Republic's purpose mirrors this vision: to create conditions in which every citizen can pursue excellence across mental, physical, spiritual, and communal dimensions. The MPL, by separating material prosperity from labor while channeling abundance equitably, removed coercion and scarcity as barriers to virtue. The accumulation of public debt, once a convenient but immoral transfer of burdens to unborn generations, became ethically indefensible once machines could bear any conceivable load. Surpluses now fund institutions dedicated to renewal: psychic research institutes exploring consciousness and non-local mind, interstellar academies training explorers and philosophers, and citizen assemblies continually refining levy rates, UHI adjustments, and allocation priorities.

The path was not without challenges, but each was met with foresight and institutional resilience. Early fears that high marginal rates would stifle innovation were addressed through generous research-and-development credits: systems that demonstrably expanded human creativity, scientific frontiers, or exploratory capacity received substantial rebates or credits against liability. Concerns about bias or capture in AGI assessors led to rigorous annual "curvature audits" employing advanced Riemannian manifold mathematics (the same toolkit used by intelligence agencies for the predictive modeling of security threats). Citizen sortition panels, rotated regularly, reviewed valuation algorithms and override protocols, ensuring the system remained the servant of the polis rather than its master. Above all, the framework preserved deliberate openness to uncertainty, leaving space for genuine creativity, miracles, and emergent phenomena that no purely deterministic model could predict.

In retrospect, the elimination of deficits and debt was never miraculous; it was the logical consequence of choosing abundance over scarcity when the technological opportunity presented itself. The Republic could have doubled down blindly on 20th-century fiscal orthodoxy — raising labor taxes, slashing entitlements, or printing money — while watching public debt spiral rapidly toward insolvency. Instead, it embraced the new reality, redesigning revenue capture around machine productivity, harnessing exponential growth, and applying surpluses with discipline and democratic deliberation. The outcome is a fiscal architecture worthy of an interstellar civilization: perpetually balanced, radically transparent, and single-mindedly dedicated to human flourishing.

The journey from $38.9 trillion in debt in 2026 to zero in 2044 was not linear but compounded at extraordinary speed. Surpluses that appeared in the late 2030s first retired the highest-interest obligations; compounding savings then accelerated principal reduction. By the early 2040s, MPL revenues generated trillions annually. Citizen referenda repeatedly favored aggressive payoff strategies, understanding that debt freedom magnified collective virtue and freed resources for higher purposes. Once the debt was gone, the annual upward calibration of UHI in step with 10–12 percent GDP growth ensured that prosperity continued compounding for every individual. Today, in 2126, the Republic's budgets project perpetual surpluses stretching into the indefinite future. Excess is channeled into voluntary citizen innovation funds, cosmic-scale expansion projects, and, most importantly, the ever-rising dividend that has come to define everyday life in the age of abundance.

This saga demonstrates that technology, when guided by wise, participatory governance, can resolve problems long considered intractable.

AGI and robotics did not merely automate production; they automated fiscal solvency, and then universal enrichment. The national debt, once viewed as an existential threat hanging over future generations, has become a minor historical footnote — a reminder that when machines produce in superabundance, the only rational, moral, and sustainable policy is to share the bounty equitably, retire the burdens of the past, and allow every citizen to grow richer, freer, and more capable of virtue with every passing year.

XI

Defending the Republic's Borders with AGI and Robotics

In the year 2126, the vast American Republic sprawls across the surface of the Earth and twenty nearby solar systems. It is the largest, most advanced state in history, and humanity's first interstellar civilization. Across this immense realm, poverty has been banished through the institution of Universal High Income, a dividend paid to US citizens, drawn from progressive levies upon the prodigious output of artificial general intelligence (AGI) systems and robotic labor. The introduction of Universal High Income (UHI) has done far more than sever the ancient link between labor and survival. It has given each American citizen an income and standard of living beyond what all but the wealthiest individuals could have imagined at the beginning of the twenty-first century.

This material abundance for all citizens has resulted from decades of double-digit GDP growth, which has grown the U.S. economy to over ninety-five quadrillion dollars. In this realm of superabundance, interstellar travel and tourism, voluntary emigration to the thriving exoplanet colonies, and unlimited AGI-facilitated education in any discipline have become accessible to every citizen. Healthcare and housing of the highest conceivable quality are likewise universally available, woven seamlessly into the fabric of daily life. What once lay in the realm of distant fantasy now sustains the everyday rhythms of existence, freeing the human spirit to pursue higher callings of creativity, discovery, and exploration.

The Republic's unprecedented abundance and dynamism are unique among the nations of the Earth. Naturally, its good fortune has not escaped the notice of those who dwell beyond its vast frontiers. America's wealth exerts a powerful gravitational pull upon the inhabitants of other, less fortunate states, some of whom, moved by an understandable longing for a share in such unprecedented bounty, seek to violate its borders as illegal economic migrants. The very technologies that produced America's superabundance — AGI and robotics — now help to preserve the sanctity of its borders, on Earth and in space.

American border defense in 2126 bears little resemblance to the fragmented and often anguished arrangements of earlier eras. It has become a seamless, living orchestration of artificial general intelligence, advanced robotics, and discerning human oversight — an intelligent membrane ensuring that every entry aligns with the laws and deeper ethos of the Republic. This approach commands broad and enduring support among the citizenry, who perceive it as vital to safeguarding the integrity of their way of life. Through neural-linked civic interfaces, polls reveal citizen support consistently surpassing ninety percent, a quiet consensus that true prosperity must be shared by following lawful pathways rather than stolen by circumventing U.S. laws. Autonomous robotic legions and drone constellations patrol the land, air, and sea borders of the U.S. with nearly flawless precision, their actions guided and reviewed by human border agents schooled in both vigilance and compassion.

Essentially all who attempt to cross into the U.S. illegally are intercepted. They are treated with dignity, processed humanely, and returned to their countries of origin expeditiously. U.S. law and public opinion in the age of UHI and revitalized citizenship have no tolerance for illegal immigration. They are free from suicidal empathy. At the same time, a thoughtfully structured legal immigration system welcomes a measured number of newcomers, each undergoing careful evaluation and immersion in the core values that animate and underpin the Republic. Any serious breach of their commitments as newly minted citizens after their naturalization will, following due process, result in revocation and deportation. Appreciating what is at stake, very few immigrants choose to violate their oath of citizenship.

To truly appreciate the refined character of border protection in 2126, one must return, with measured reflection, to the more turbulent patterns of former times. The evolution of these defenses echoes wider movements within society under the influence of Universal High Income. In the centuries before widespread automation, borders often stood as arenas of raw desperation. Deep economic imbalances drove men, women, and children to risk their very lives on dangerous journeys in search of a better life. National responses swayed uneasily between the impulses of compassion and the imperatives of security, vacillating between occasional amnesties on one hand, and building physical barriers and toughening border enforcement on the other.

During the late twentieth and early twenty-first centuries, America's borders were guarded by an uneven patchwork: physical fences and walls, vehicle and foot patrols, and early forms of electronic surveillance. The southern frontier with Mexico, spanning more than nineteen hundred miles of varied and demanding terrain, became a focal point of contention, marked by barriers, surveillance towers, and dedicated agents of the Customs and Border Protection service. Along the coasts, the Coast Guard deployed vessels and aircraft to interdict seaborne approaches. Yet these measures suffered from inherent limitations. Immense stretches of land remained difficult to monitor continuously; human agents endured physical danger, fatigue, and psychological strain; and resourceful smuggling networks repeatedly discovered and exploited gaps in security. Annual unauthorized crossings reached into the millions at times, placing heavy burdens upon public resources and deepening domestic political divides. The 2020s brought further intensification as the Covid pandemic and economic shocks sent waves of migrants and refugees toward the U.S. borders, overwhelming existing facilities and at times giving rise to humanitarian crises.

The turning point arrived with the emergence of true AGI and sophisticated robotics in the first third of the twenty-first century, leading to the rollout of Universal High Income (UHI) in 2036. As machines took over many forms of routine mental and physical labor, economic productivity soared and the U.S. achieved unprecedented levels of growth. Yet the very success of its economy intensified the magnetic pull it exerted far beyond its borders. Analytical projections from early AGI systems foresaw illegal crossing attempts climbing toward twenty million annually by 2045. In response, the Border Renaissance Initiative was launched — an ambitious, multi-trillion-dollar endeavor financed through revenues derived from robotic and AGI productivity. The initiative deliberately reduced reliance upon human border patrol agents while dramatically improving detection and response capabilities by leveraging both AGI and advanced robotics. Early experimental systems, such as the DroneNet deployed in 2046, demonstrated the new system's potential by cutting unauthorized incursions in half within a few years. Formal legislation, notably the Border Integrity Act of 2048, embedded AGI coordination into national policy, moving the entire framework from a posture of reaction toward one of thoughtful anticipation.

Skeptics at the time voiced understandable concern that such technologies might erode human control of the border and transform the public image of the Republic overseas into that of a cold, impenetrable fortress. In practice, however, the system matured into something more balanced: a humane and highly effective guardian that drew upon AGI's capacity for foresight and the tireless, precise action of robots, all kept within an ethical horizon based on Asimov's Laws and maintained by human judgment. By 2126, borders have transcended their former status as mere lines drawn upon maps. They function instead as dynamic, responsive perimeters — intelligent, conscious fields that adapt fluidly to shifting conditions while consistently honoring the dignity inherent in every person. The Republic's incorporation of new territories from time to time has been followed by the seamless extension of this conscious system of border protection, from the mountains of Armenia to the Arctic Ocean.

At the heart of this living system resides a constellation of AGI-directed robotic forces that together form a resilient and adaptive protective field. AGI, having evolved far beyond the narrow neural architectures of the early 2020s into fully self-aware intelligences endowed with refined ethical discernment, serves as the central orchestrator. Asimov's Three Laws form a key part of their cognitive structure. These minds, safeguarded within quantum-secured data sanctuaries, continuously contemplate vast streams of information drawn from satellite observations, environmental sensors, encrypted global communications, and subtle social media indicators. Through algorithms attuned to predictive empathy — insights drawn from deeper understandings of consciousness and motivation — AGI anticipates not only the timing and scale of potential migratory movements but the underlying human circumstances that give rise to them. Should patterns suggest impending famine in Central America or displacement driven by shifting climatic conditions, the system may quietly position humanitarian aid drones near likely approach corridors, offering assistance before desperation fully compels a mass crossing. Similarly, early signals of unrest detected through carefully monitored global feeds allow the preemptive deployment of resources to the borders, for example to Greenland's remote northern reaches, where melting ice has gradually opened previously impassable migration routes.

The robotic guardians themselves display remarkable adaptability and responsiveness. Humanoid and quadrupedal units, crafted by innovative enterprises such as xAI Robotics, move across the landscape with quiet competence. Equipped with both non-lethal and lethal weaponry, they prioritize de-escalation. The Sentinel series, for example, stands approximately two meters in height and features modular configurations: desert-adapted models draw continuous power from flexible solar skins, while Arctic variants incorporate thermal shielding and reinforced treads suited to Greenland's tundra and glacial fields. Their movements reveal a graceful agility far beyond ordinary human limits, allowing effortless traversal of mountains, forests, deserts, and frozen expanses alike.

Most striking is the quality of interaction made possible by their integrated AGI cores. Upon encountering illegal migrants, these machines project holographic guides and speak fluently in any of several hundred languages and dialects, offering clear explanations of legal avenues, providing immediate water or medical attention, and extending gestures of basic kindness. Quadrupedal companions, evoking the sure-footedness of canines yet enhanced by advanced sensors, range ahead into broken terrain. They detect concealed presences through refined olfactory arrays, auditory sensors, and hyperspectral vision. Specialized cold-climate versions keep watch over Greenland's frozen frontiers.

Complementing these ground forces, layered aerial and maritime elements complete the protective field. Swarms of diminutive drones, no larger than hummingbirds, maintain an almost constant watchful presence, channeling detailed visual and spectral data back to central AGI nodes. Larger vertical-takeoff craft deploy precision containment fields that can envelop groups with minimal physical intrusion, shepherding them gently toward designated processing areas. Along the Republic's extensive coastlines, autonomous submersibles and surface vessels glide through the waters. These marine units, animated by fusion power sources, employ bio-inspired propulsion that mimics the fluid grace of sea creatures, granting them stealth and endurance. Advanced sonar and quantum radar pierce any attempts at concealment by human traffickers.

Throughout all border operations, human judgment retains its essential central role, ensuring that technology remains the servant of the citizens rather than their master. Border agents, few in number yet exceptionally trained and prepared, operate from augmented-reality command centers scattered across the Republic's territories. Their training at the Border Academy cultivates moral sensitivity through immersive ethical simulations. Neural enhancements and exosuits amplify their physical and cognitive reach without diminishing their humanity. Direct interfaces allow agents to engage with AGI recommendations and, when deeper ethical considerations arise, to have the final say. Every significant decision is recorded upon immutable distributed ledgers, preserving transparency for future reflection and accountability. This balanced partnership — AGI offering breadth and tireless precision, humans contributing empathy and wisdom — has yielded striking results. Since 2060, no border agent has suffered fatal injury in the line of duty, while the overall rate of successful interdiction stands at 99.8 percent according to rigorously verified AGI assessments.

A representative encounter illustrates the system's character. When AGI detects a caravan drawing near the Arizona frontier or a vessel approaching Greenland's eastern fjords, it dispatches scouting elements with minimal disruption. Drones observe from a respectful distance; robotic units approach with calm authority, initiating communication that offers clear information and immediate practical help. Human overseers review the unfolding events in real time, guiding outcomes that may include health screenings, consideration of credible asylum claims, or orderly repatriation. Those returned travel via efficient automated hyperloops or sub-orbital shuttles, avoiding the need for large detention centers on U.S. territory.

The deeper strength of this border architecture arises from its resonance with the wider societal transformation brought about by the AGI revolution and Universal High Income. Citizens who enjoy genuine material security tend to view the preservation of the polis and its material abundance not as a means of excluding others but as a way of protecting their own rights and those of their fellow citizens. Periodic public referenda, secured by blockchain verification and enjoying near-universal participation, consistently reaffirm the existing policies. This broad alignment encourages ongoing private-sector creativity in defense technologies, steadily lowering costs and enhancing adaptability, including specialized solutions for challenging sections of the border. Voices advocating completely open borders, though present on the libertarian margins of society, remain limited in influence, met not by dismissal but by the steady accumulation of evidence demonstrating that ordered boundaries help sustain the very abundance that benefits all citizens.

Legal migration continues to serve as the generous and principled counterpart to these protective measures. Annual immigration quotas, currently numbering around five hundred thousand, shift according to AGI projections of demographic balance, economic opportunity, and the future outflow of migrants to the Moon, Mars, and the exoplanet colonies. In 2125, for instance, the ceiling was raised by ten percent to accommodate demand from the exoplanet settlements and Alberta. Prospective entrants must pass a multi-layered assessment: preliminary virtual dialogues explore skills, intentions, and alignment with core Republican ideals such as individual responsibility, fidelity to law, and a spirit of innovation. Those who advance participate in immersive virtual-reality experiences and, if selected, attend month-long Polis Academies. These programs weave together reflective study of constitutional history—from the vision of the Founding Fathers onward—with practical engagement in the principles of Universal High Income and the ethical stewardship of powerful artificial intelligences. Naturalization concludes with a solemn citizenship oath, its sincerity gently verified through neural linkage, yielding an overall success rate of approximately 98 percent.

Once admitted, new citizens receive immediate access to Universal High Income and full opportunities for participation. Yet the Republic maintains gentle but firm safeguards. Continuous, privacy-respecting AGI monitoring of civic patterns helps identify rare instances of serious misalignment, such as criminal conduct or active opposition to foundational polis commitments. When such cases arise, they proceed through transparent trials before juries augmented by impartial AGI analysis. Sanctions initially emphasize rehabilitation through constructive public service, rather than punishment. Denaturalization and deportation remain the final option, providing the system with necessary rigor. A documented 2124 episode, in which a naturalized individual sought to incite widespread resistance to AGI systems, followed this path: after due process, the former immigrant was stripped of his citizenship and repatriated to his homeland. Such outcomes remain uncommon, accounting for a fraction of one percent of all immigrants.

Environmental and geopolitical realities continue to present evolving tests. Rising sea levels reshape coastlines, while the gradual opening of Arctic passages near Greenland introduces new potential corridors of movement. The AGI framework responds by continuously refining perimeter configurations, ensuring adaptability without rigidity. Those who seek to circumvent the system through jamming technologies or other countermeasures encounter defenses that evolve more swiftly still, fortified by quantum encryption and iterative innovation. International critics occasionally press for fewer border restrictions, and the Republic responds primarily through expansive foreign assistance programs that share insights and models for fostering localized versions of abundance. Within the Republic itself, thoughtful debates persist regarding the proper boundaries of predictive intelligence in human affairs. Annual independent audits, coupled with explicit human override protocols, guard against overreach and preserve the system's ethical center.

The same underlying principles scale gracefully into the Republic's extraterrestrial domains. Lunar and Martian settlements, housed beneath protective domes and engaged in resource stewardship, confront occasional unauthorized approaches from rival entities or independent actors — sometimes labeled "void migrants" or, on Mars, "dust devils," who attempt to exploit atmospheric storms for cover. Orbital sentinels, seismic arrays, and agile drone networks maintain watch. Upon the exoplanets, natural features such as gravitational gradients serve as helpful complements to rings of guardian satellites and faster-than-light sensor arrays capable of detecting unsanctioned warp arrivals. Across vast distances, AGI maintains coherence through quantum entanglement relays, ensuring that the spirit of the polis remains undivided. Legal migration to the colonies is possible only after ten years of residence in the Republic's core terrestrial territories. In this way, the framework of ordered abundance extends without fracture across both Earth and the cosmos.

In the final analysis, the Republic's border defenses in 2126 represent far more than a mechanism for controlling population movements. They stand as a mature expression of the polis ideal itself: an intelligent and harmonious system in which advanced technology serves the fuller unfolding of human life, sovereignty safeguards the citizens' prosperity, and a spirit of ordered generosity informs all interactions on the border with would-be migrants.

Through the thoughtful integration of artificial general intelligence, responsive robotics, and attuned human presence, the Republic defends its borders with firmness and compassion, free from the delusions of suicidal empathy.

XII

The New Hoplites

In the year 2126, the military forces of the United States form a vast and lethal armada stretching from the Republic's terrestrial heartland to its lunar outposts, Martian settlements, and the 20 thriving exoplanet colonies. This extensive domain, secured by a seamless integration of Artificial General Intelligence (AGI), advanced robotics, and a force of citizen soldiers liberated from want by Universal High Income (UHI), reflects a profound evolution from the conventional armed forces of a century prior. The Republic's military is a precise, ethical, and overwhelmingly lethal force, focused on deterrence, exploration, and the preservation of polis values on Earth and in the cosmos.

UHI, the unconditional dividend funded by progressive taxation on AI and robotic productivity, has decoupled military service from economic necessity, transforming it into a voluntary pursuit based on duty and honor. AGI directs military operations, from cyber attacks to UAV deployments, with superhuman efficiency. Robotics, once represented by rudimentary drones, now takes the form of legions of adaptable machines which execute missions with minimal human risk. Human judgment is integrated into all levels of decision-making, with the last word always resting with human commanders. Together, these elements have reshaped the military from a labor-intensive force into a symbiotic human-machine alliance, ensuring the Republic's security while upholding its ethos of individual freedom and universal prosperity.

Central to this transformation is the revival of citizenship in the political model of the revived polis, which has profoundly altered and strengthened the bond between the citizenry and their all-volunteer military. In the pre-UHI era, true citizenship had withered away, becoming a mere legal status conferring rights without demanding much in the way of active participation. Moreover, the expansion of both state and corporate power had whittled down the rights of citizenship over the years. The adoption of DEI and Woke doctrines by some corporations stifled free speech. As a result, most citizens thought of themselves as employees and consumers first and citizens second. Incredibly, half of American citizens did not even bother to vote, and those who wished to do so received no time off to go to the polls, since Election Day was not yet a federal holiday.

Military service, while voluntary since the 1970s, was frequently motivated by economic incentives or educational benefits, creating a professional military class detached from broader American society. Less than one percent of the population served in the military. Most citizens had no conception of the importance or hardships of military service, and only the crudest conception of the Republic's security interests. The revival of the polis ideal, inspired by ancient Athens and adapted to current realities, has redefined citizenship as requiring an active, engaged role in governance and society. Freed from the need to devote most of their time and energy to survival, Americans now build their lives around the concept of citizenship. They participate in neural-linked assemblies, vote on key policies via blockchain-secured referenda, and contribute to communal decisions, fostering a sense of shared ownership over the Republic's destiny. Although the U.S. military is an elite force, not a mass conscription army, all citizens undergo basic military for a year at age 18, as part of the process of assuming the rights and duties of citizenship. Thereafter they serve in reserve units until the age of 50.

This is so because the revival of citizenship has been accompanied by a profound resurgence of the ancient idea of the "hoplite" or citizen-soldier who bears arms in defense of the polis, embodying the inseparability of civic duty and martial responsibility. In classical Athens, the hoplite was not a professional warrior but an ordinary citizen — a farmer, artisan, or, in the case of Socrates, a philosopher — who equipped himself at personal expense and stood shoulder-to-shoulder with fellow citizens in the phalanx, a formation that symbolized the collective solidarity and mutual dependence of the military community. This model reinforced the polis's democratic ethos: only those willing to risk their lives for the community could fully participate in its governance. In 2126, this hoplite ideal has been reborn, adapted to an era of abundance and technology. UHI eliminates the financial barriers that once limited such participation, allowing every citizen to "arm" themselves not with bronze shields but with knowledge, neural enhancements, and voluntary service commitments. Military service is seen as one of the ultimate expression of citizenship, a rite that harkens back to the phalanx's discipline while integrating AGI and robotics as modern "allies" in the line.

The example of Socrates poignantly illustrates this revived paradigm. In ancient Athens, Socrates — the founder of Western philosophy — served as a hoplite in several campaigns, including the battles of Potidaea (432-429 BC), Amphipolis (422 BC), and Delium (424 BC). Despite his intellectual pursuits and sharp critiques of Athenian society, Socrates fulfilled his civic duty with mastery and enthusiasm, fighting in the phalanx where his steadfastness and skill saved the life of Alcibiades at Potidaea and earned praise for his courage. Plato's dialogues, such as the Symposium and Laches, depict Socrates as a model citizen-soldier, whose military service complemented his philosophical inquiries into virtue, justice, and the good life. This integration of thought and action exemplified both the hoplite ethos and the ideals of otium and eudaemonia: citizenship demanded not only deliberation in the assembly but readiness to defend the polis physically.

In the American Republic of 2126, this Socratic model resonates deeply. Citizens, freed by UHI to pursue pursuits akin to Socrates' philosophical inquiries, view military service as a key expression of citizenship. School curricula emphasize Classical history, and immersive AGI simulations recreate Delium's chaos, with participants observing Socrates' lethal focus in the tumult of combat. Such training fosters a cultural reverence for the "hoplite-citizen," whose voluntary service is celebrated as a philosophical act. The revival of polis ideals strengthens the citizen-military bond by framing service as a personal and collective quest for virtue, ensuring that the military remains accountable to a populace that sees itself as potential hoplites, ready to stand in defense of abundance and freedom.

No longer is the military seen as a distant institution; it is an extension of the polis itself. Citizens, secure in UHI's abundance, view military service not as a sacrifice but as a noble expression of civic virtue. Annual polis forums dedicate sessions to military strategy, where ordinary citizens — artists, educators, entrepreneurs — debate deployment ethics, technological integrations, and terrestrial and interstellar defense priorities. This participatory model strengthens public trust in the military: polls conducted via neural interfaces show approval rates for the Republic's military policy exceeding 95%. The all-volunteer military, drawn from this engaged populace, embodies the polis ideal — as the defenders of the Republic, they are also thinkers, innovators, and guardians of polis values.

Recruitment into this all-volunteer force is deliberately selective and meritocratic, reflecting the government's commitment to excellence and civic responsibility rather than mass mobilization. With Universal High Income ensuring that no citizen serves out of economic desperation, the active-duty military draws exclusively from those who have already completed their mandatory one-year basic training at age 18 and demonstrated exceptional leadership potential during their reserve service. The total human complement stands at approximately 100,000 personnel—every one of them a commissioned officer or noncommissioned officer. There are no junior enlisted ranks in the traditional sense; robotic systems and embedded AGI handle the labor-intensive, high-risk tasks once performed by the bulk of military manpower. This structure ensures that every human in uniform possesses the education, ethical grounding, and command authority required to direct autonomous forces in an era where a single officer can oversee the equivalent of an entire 20th-century brigade.

Prospective officers and NCOs apply through a rigorous, polis-wide selection process that begins with recommendations from local citizen assemblies and culminates in competitive examinations administered at the revived legacy military academies. West Point, Annapolis, the Air Force Academy, and the newly established Space and Exoplanet Warfare College in Colorado Springs have all been modernized while preserving their historic campuses and traditions. Classrooms once filled with blackboards now feature immersive neural-interface simulators capable of replicating the fog of ground combat or the gravitational anomalies of exoplanet operations. Cadets still march in formation on the Plain at West Point, but their drills now integrate synchronized movements with platoons of humanoid and quadrupedal robots, teaching the seamless choreography of human oversight. The curriculum blends classical military history — Thucydides and Clausewitz remain required reading — with cutting-edge disciplines: AGI ethics, neural augmentation protocols, multi-domain command theory, and the philosophy of just war in an age of abundance. Graduates emerge not merely as tacticians but as philosopher-warriors in the Socratic mold, capable of balancing lethal precision with the moral imperatives of the Republic.

Upon commissioning, a typical officer's career begins at the platoon level, the fundamental building block of the modern force. A standard platoon comprises one human first lieutenant, one human sergeant, and roughly 100 robotic combatants—roughly sixty bipedal humanoid platforms for complex urban or exoplanet operations, thirty quadrupedal units optimized for rugged terrain and heavy fire support, and a complement of airborne micro-drones and aquatic submersibles for reconnaissance and precision strikes. All platforms are linked through a dedicated unit-level AGI battle advisor, a distributed intelligence that processes sensor data from every robot, predicts enemy movements with 99.8 percent accuracy in simulations, and offers real-time tactical recommendations. Yet the human officers retain absolute final authority. Through neural implants and augmented-reality sensor displays integrated into their combat suits, the lieutenant and sergeant maintain complete awareness of the entire battlespace. They issue commands via thought alone, override AGI suggestions instantaneously when need be, and can experience the sensory feed of every robot as an extension of their own perception. This intimate human-machine symbiosis turns the platoon into a single, thinking organism — lethal, adaptable, and ethically anchored by human judgment.

Training emphasizes mastery of this command relationship. Early academy courses focus on basic robot handling in controlled environments, progressing to full-spectrum exercises that replicate contested troop insertions, undersea engagements, or surface operations on exoplanets with hostile atmospheres and exotic biologies. Cadets learn to trust their AGI advisors while cultivating the intellectual discipline to question them when polis values or strategic nuance demand it. Peace-time rotations alternate between Earth-based deterrence patrols and forward deployments to the twenty exoplanet colonies, where officers command mixed human-robot garrisons protecting terraform domes and mining outposts. Combat training, conducted almost entirely in hyper-realistic AGI simulations to minimize risk, stresses rapid decision-making under uncertainty and fire. Officers practice scenarios ranging from punitive raids against unruly terrestrial powers to boarding actions against rogue starships. The goal is not rote obedience but cultivated wisdom — the ability to wield overwhelming robotic force with precision and maximum effect.

As officers advance in rank, their responsibilities and neural augmentations scale accordingly. Captains commanding companies —

typically four platoons — receive enhanced neural lattices that allow simultaneous oversight of four hundred robots across multiple domains. Majors and lieutenant colonels, leading battalions, undergo further augmentation enabling coordination of several thousand platforms, integrating ground, air, sea, and orbital assets into unified operations. At the general officer level, command extends to entire theaters: a single four-star admiral might direct a solar-system-wide fleet comprising hundreds of thousands of robotic vessels while receiving layered advice from theater-level battle intelligences. These senior leaders, often in their fifties after decades of service, embody the apex of the hoplite-citizen ideal — battle-hardened yet philosophically attuned, their neural enhancements calibrated to amplify rather than replace human cognition and intuition. Promotion boards, composed of peers and civilian polis representatives, evaluate not only tactical brilliance but ethical consistency and civic engagement, ensuring the officer corps remains representative of the Republic's values.

The Republic's military forces encompass a diverse array of platforms tailored to the multi-domain realities of 2126. On land, legions of agile quadrupedal and humanoid robots, supported by autonomous armored vehicles, provide overwhelming ground presence with zero human casualties in routine operations. Naval forces include crewless surface ships and submersibles patrolling Earth's oceans, as well as the subsurface hydrospheres of distant moons. Air and orbital wings deploy swarms of hypersonic drones and stealth satellites capable of global strike within minutes. Beyond Earth, the fleet incorporates warp-drive vessels — sleek, AGI-piloted starships capable of traversing the solar system in hours and reaching the exoplanet colonies in weeks. Every interstellar transport and colony ship carries a dedicated military detachment: a reinforced battalion of officers and robots tasked with safeguarding the Republic's lines of communication against piracy, natural disasters, or hostile interference. These detachments ensure that the many-stranded web of trade, migration, and cultural exchange binding the Republic to its far-flung possessions remains intact.

Operationally, the regular military's primary missions remain deterrence against other terrestrial powers and swift intervention in hotspots where Republic interests or polis principles are threatened. Forward-deployed robotic task forces, commanded by small human teams, maintain a constant presence along contested borders and trade routes, projecting power without the massive logistical burdens of massed human troops. When crises erupt — whether a rival power's attempt to seize an asteroid mining claim or an ideological insurgency in the EU successor states — human commanders authorize precise, proportionate responses. AGI battle advisors model thousands of outcomes in seconds, but officers weigh the ethical calculus: civilian risk, long-term stability, and fidelity to republican values. This human-in-t he-loop doctrine prevents the unchecked escalation that pure machine autonomy might invite, preserving the moral legitimacy that underpins the polis.

Crucially, the regular military does not handle domestic border security, a function reserved for the separate Border Forces. This distinction, enshrined in the amended Constitution, prevents the militarization of civilian life and reinforces the principle that the armed forces exist solely for external defense and the protection of free movement within the polis domain. The Border Forces focus on border defense, immigration processing, and customs enforcement, including counter-smuggling operations.

The integration of AGI and robotics into military operations has elevated the human element; it has elevated it. Officers command with a clarity and confidence unimaginable in earlier eras, their neural implants converting terabytes of battlefield data into intuitive understanding. A lieutenant on a counter-terrorism deployment can direct a hundred robots to rescue trapped citizens while simultaneously neutralizing the terrorist threat, all while consulting his AGI battle advisor and retaining veto power over any potential escalation proposed by the AGI. This command philosophy, rooted in Socratic self-examination, ensures that technology serves citizenship rather than supplanting it. Annual after-action reviews, conducted in polis assemblies via neural link, allow citizens to scrutinize major operations, fostering transparency and continuous ethical refinement.

In peacetime, the military contributes actively to Republic life beyond deterrence. Robotic engineering corps, under officer supervision, assist in terraforming projects on exoplanets and disaster relief on Earth. Cultural exchange programs rotate officers through civilian polis forums, where they share insights on military tactics and strategy and receive feedback from their fellow citizens. This permeability between the military and civilian spheres strengthens the hoplite ideal: service is not a cloistered profession but an expression of civic virtue. After their military careers are over, many officers return to civilian life as leaders in business, academia, or governance.

The scale of the force — modest in comparison to the pre-AGI military yet global and interstellar in reach — exemplifies the efficiency of the UHI era. Where once millions of soldiers were required for global dominance, 100,000 highly trained officers now command an armada whose robotic components number over ten million. This lean structure frees resources for exploration, scientific research, and the enrichment of polis culture. Yet its lethality remains unmatched; simulations show that a single reinforced brigade could neutralize threats that would have required entire armies a century earlier. Deterrence is maintained not through sheer mass but through demonstrated precision, ethical restraint, and the visible commitment of the citizen-officers who embody the Republic's highest ideals.

As the Republic expands ever farther in the cosmos, the military's role evolves from guardian of Earth to steward of humanity's cosmic destiny. On the exoplanets, officers oversee joint human-robot bases, where they train local citizen militias in basic command protocols so that each colony can defend itself while remaining integrated into the Republic's command network. Interstellar patrols respond to distress calls across light-years, their warp-drive vessels carrying mobile command nodes that allow flag officers to direct operations in distant solar systems from the bridge while maintaining contact with the Department of War back on Earth. This far-flung posture demands not only technological sophistication but a renewed emphasis on the virtues of patience, foresight, and solidarity — the very qualities Socrates modeled in the phalanx.

The U.S. military of 2126 is a force where technology amplifies human excellence rather than replacing it, where citizenship and service are inseparable, and where the ancient hoplite's shield has now become a neural link and legions of loyal machines. In an age of abundance, the Republic's defenders prove that true security flows not from fear or coercion but from the enlightened consent of a free people ready to command the future. As citizens debate the next generation of warp-drive propulsion or the ethical limits of combat AGI, they do so with the quiet confidence that their military — small in number, but nearly infinite in capability — will remain the faithful instrument of their collective will. The phalanx endures, reborn in silicon and starlight, ensuring that the Republic's light continues to shine across space and time.

XIII

Trading With the Lesser Powers

In the year 2126, the United States stands not merely as a nation but as humanity's first interstellar civilization, whose economic might defies all historical precedent. With a Gross Domestic Product surpassing 95 quadrillion dollars, sustained by the relentless exponential growth of 12 percent annually since the AGI breakthrough, the American polis operates on a scale that renders the economies of every other terrestrial power almost comically diminutive. By contrast, the European Union's successor states, the Russian Federation, the fragmented successors to the Chinese People's Republic, India, and the nations of Latin America have economies measured in mere billions or trillions. This chasm is no accident of geography or resources; it is the direct consequence of America's early and decisive embrace of artificial general intelligence, humanoid robotics, and the Alcubierre Drive. While other societies hesitated, regulated, or fragmented under the pressures of the late 21st century, the United States integrated these forces seamlessly into its revised political system, achieving superabundance, decoupling prosperity from labor through Universal High Income, and extending its reach to the solar system and twenty thriving exoplanets.

This economic supremacy manifests most visibly in America's trade posture toward the rest of Earth. The United States maintains a colossal and perpetual trade surplus with the entire globe, exporting far more in value than it imports even as its citizens enjoy standards of living that would have seemed utopian mere decades earlier. Yet this surplus is exercised with characteristic American restraint and foresight. Federal legislation, reinforced by citizen oversight boards, strictly controls the export of core high-technology goods, particularly AGI architectures, advanced humanoid robotics platforms, Riemannian manifold neural systems, and components enabling Alcubierre warp drive propulsion. These technologies remain the guarded inheritance of the American people, available only under the most tightly audited licensing regimes to the closest allies and even then only in sanitized, non-replicable forms. The guiding principle is simple and rooted in the adapted Asimovian safeguards embedded in every American AGI system: protect humanity's liberty and prevent any risk that uncontrolled proliferation might destabilize the delicate balance of abundance and self-governance that defines the polis.

What the United States does export in abundance are the fruits of that controlled technological edge: robot-manufactured consumer goods produced at negligible marginal cost, hyper-efficient agricultural and pharmaceutical products, holographic entertainment and cultural media that captivate global audiences, limited-tier automation tools that enhance rather than supplant human labor, clean-energy solutions derived from solar-plus-battery systems, and access to space-derived resources funneled through the colonies. Imports, by contrast, consist overwhelmingly of those irreplaceable human touches that even the most sophisticated AGI cannot fully replicate — artisanal foods and wines, traditional crafts infused with generational cultural memory, unique biodiversity samples for research, luxury textiles and fashion, and the creative output of Earth's still-scarcity-driven artists and thinkers. The interstellar colonies themselves amplify this dynamic; fully 15 percent of U.S. GDP flows through warp-enabled trade with the exoplanets, yet the surplus with Earth remains so vast that terrestrial commerce, though modest in percentage terms, still measures in the quadrillions and serves as a stabilizing force for the entire planet.

Underpinning this framework is the philosophical architecture of the polis itself. Every trade treaty is debated in local assemblies, modeled by AGI advisory councils for optimal outcomes, and ultimately ratified by Congress. The result is commerce that feels less like exploitation and more like benevolent patronage: an extension of the otium and eudaemonia that define American life, offered as an invitation for other societies to glimpse the possibilities of post-scarcity existence without handing them the keys to replicate it prematurely. The U.S. dollar reigns supreme, accepted everywhere on Earth and backed by the nearly infinite productivity of American robotics and AGI. Deflationary pressures within the U.S. economy mean that even the smallest trade inflows purchase enormous volumes of Earth's output, while American exports flood global markets at prices that undercut any local competition yet still generate handsome returns for U.S. shareholders. In this manner, trade becomes both an instrument of soft power and living proof that the American experiment in its current form offers the last, best hope of mankind.

The former states of the European Union, now a loose, quarrelsome confederation of sovereign nations bound by cultural affinity and shared history rather than a single, neo-imperial political entity, are some of America's closest terrestrial trading partners. Decades of cautious regulation in the 2030s and 2040s, combined with lingering skepticism toward unchecked AGI development, left these nations—France, Germany, Italy, Spain, the Nordic countries, and the rest—trapped in economies still measured in the mere billions or trillions. Their combined output barely registers as a rounding error against the quadrillion-scale U.S. economy. Yet the relationship is one of profound mutual respect, tinged with sympathy, echoing the lingering historical and cultural ties between the American colossus and the elderly nations of Europe.

American exports to the former EU states flow in an unceasing torrent of abundance. Holographic entertainment libraries, produced by sentiment-aware AGI collaborators and broadcast via quantum-secured channels, dominate European leisure time. Non-sentient household fabricators, capable of on-demand manufacturing of clothing, furniture, and small appliances but deliberately barred from full robotic autonomy or self-replication, fill European homes at prices that make local industry obsolete. Hyper-efficient agricultural goods, grown in American vertical farms tended by tireless humanoid robots, supply fruits and vegetables of astonishing quality, driving European food prices to historic lows. Limited medical technologies, such as advanced diagnostic scanners and regenerative therapies that stop short of true AGI-driven personalization, flow under strict licensing. Most visibly, the United States offers subsidized access to interstellar tourism: warp-enabled voyages to lunar resorts, Martian outposts, and even short layovers on the nearest exoplanet colonies, experiences that have become the ultimate status symbol for the European elites and middle classes alike. Sport exchanges add another layer; European athletes compete in American-led interstellar leagues, their teams equipped with AI-augmented but non-sentient training gear, fostering goodwill and cultural exchange.

In return, America imports the very soul of European civilization. French wines and cheeses, produced by human hands in traditional vineyards and aging cellars untouched by robotic intervention, command premium prices among U.S. citizens seeking authenticity. Italian fashion houses, still reliant on human designers and artisans, supply the U.S. with garments that blend centuries-old craftsmanship with subtle American smart-fabric enhancements. German precision machinery — now quaint by U.S. standards but prized for its human-engineered elegance — finds its way into specialty applications. Cultural artifacts, from Renaissance paintings to live orchestral performances streamed in real time, enrich American otium. Biodiversity samples from the Alps and Mediterranean, pharmaceutical formulations rooted in traditional herbal knowledge, and even tourism services (Europeans hosting American visitors in historic cities) round out the import ledger.

The result is a trade surplus measured in the hundreds of trillions annually—enormous for the European side, negligible for America, yet profoundly stabilizing. European nations have begun quietly adopting elements of the UHI model in pilot programs, funded in part by trade revenues. Polis-style sortition has appeared in several municipal governments. Old fears of American cultural imperialism have dissolved; instead, some Europeans now view the relationship as a gentle bridge toward eventual post-scarcity. Strict American controls ensure that no core AGI or robotics technology leaks across the Atlantic, preserving the technological gap while allowing Europe to thrive at its own pace. In the grand mosaic of U.S. foreign policy, the former EU states are not vassals but cherished cousins, their contributions preserving the human element that even curvature-based artificial minds cannot fully replicate.

Relations with the Russian Federation, a stable and resource-rich power that weathered the 21st-century transitions through pragmatic authoritarian continuity, follow a pattern of respectful pragmatism. Russia's economy, still measured in the low trillions despite its vast territory and mineral wealth, stands in stark contrast to the American behemoth. Yet trade flows smoothly, facilitated by the mutual recognition that neither side seeks domination over the other.

American exports emphasize abundance without threat. Consumer goods — clothing, electronics, and household items churned out by robotic factories — arrive via conventional shipping augmented by orbital drop pods for more exclusive items. They are priced so low that they raise Russian living standards significantly. Advanced medical technologies and clean-energy kits (solar arrays and battery storage systems deliberately capped below full

American efficiency) help modernize Russian infrastructure. Holographic sports broadcasts and entertainment libraries introduce Russian citizens to the vibrancy of American entertainment, while educational content, stripped of advanced AGI tutoring modules, finds eager audiences in Russian universities. Most strategically, the United States offers access to off-world resources, such as rare isotopes mined from colonial asteroids, under long-term contracts that stabilize the Russian energy and manufacturing sectors without transferring any warp or robotics know-how.

Russia, in turn, supplies the American polis with the treasures of the Earth. Siberian timber and minerals and specialty metals flow westward in volumes that would once have strained global supply chains but now represent mere drops in the American ocean of abundance. Caviar, vodka, and traditional foodstuffs — produced by human hands in time-honored fashion — grace American tables as exotic symbols of otium. Cultural exports, from literature and ballet to folk art, enrich the polis's philosophical discourse. Russian craftsmanship, particularly in jewelry, furniture, and precision optics, finds premium markets among citizens who value the human touch.

The trade surplus tilts heavily American, yet Russia benefits enormously. Revenues from mineral exports fund modest UHI-style stipends in pilot regions, easing the transition away from extractive labor. American oversight ensures no prohibited technologies reach Russian soil; every shipment is audited by citizen boards and quantum-secured. Geopolitical tensions that once defined the relationship have faded into history, replaced by a quiet understanding: Russia provides the raw materials of Earth, America the abundance of AGI and the stars. Both sides benefit from this admittedly unequal partnership.

The fragmentation of the former Chinese People's Republic in the late 2050s, precipitated by declining demographics, internal political convulsions, and the uneven pressures of early AGI adoption, created a mosaic of successor states: prosperous coastal enclaves, inland resource powers, and semi-autonomous regional entities. Their combined economies remain locked in the trillions, a pale shadow of what unified China might have achieved had it followed the American path. Of course, China could not follow America's path with respect to the adoption of AGI and robotics. Adoption of an economic and political model based upon restraining AGI's ability to harm the citizenry through Asimov's law did not rhyme with the Communist Party's rule book. Neither did the distribution of a high income to each citizen. In the last analysis, China failed to follow the American path toward superabundance precisely because it had no citizens, only a billion slaves, ruled over by a small ruling class of apparatchiks.

As the U.S. economy boomed after 2036, registering double-digit GDP growth every year, the terms of Sino-American trade shifted dramatically and permanently. China's trade surplus vis-a-vis the U.S. rapidly shrank and then became a permanent deficit, limited only by China's protectionist measures. The People's Republic could not withstand such a profound geopolitical shock. It was further weakened by the introduction of strict immigration and border control in the U.S., enhanced by AGI and robotics. These measures largely ended China's highly successful efforts to steal the intellectual property of U.S. high technology firms. The economic crisis of the mid-21st century laid bare a truth the international community had long chosen to ignore: much of China's economic success was based upon its parasitical trade and investment relationship with the United States.

Once this ended abruptly after 2036, the internal collapse of China was foreordained. Washington handled these developments with admirable restraint, much as it had done during the collapse of the Soviet Union 75 years previously. It gradually re-established diplomatic relations with the Chinese successor states, and then carefully wove a web of consular, economic, and security agreements with them, designed to reinforce its new dominance without advertising the fact.

American trade policy toward the successor states is the most carefully calibrated aspect of the Republic's global trade strategy, reflecting a commitment to benevolent economic uplift without risking technological leakage through the renewed theft of intellectual property. Exports from the United States are voluminous yet strictly tiered. Consumer fabricators and mid-level automation tools — capable of boosting local manufacturing but incapable of self-replication or true AGI cognition — flood the coastal states. Agricultural and pharmaceutical products alleviate food and health pressures across all the fragments of former China. Holographic media and cultural content subtly introduce American polis values of direct democracy, eudaemonia, and otium. Tourism packages to American colonies serve as both an economic stimulus and soft-power vector. Critically, no full robotics platforms, no Riemannian AGI cores, and no warp-related technologies may be exported to former China. Licensing regimes enforced by the Federal Technology Safeguard Agency ensure compliance through hardware-level quantum locks and regular citizen audits.

In return, America imports a rich tapestry of goods that only human-scale, scarcity-driven societies can still produce with competitive quality. Textiles and consumer electronics components assembled by skilled human labor in the coastal regions arrive in vast quantities, their low cost a boon to American deflation. Traditional medicines, herbal formulations, and biodiversity samples from the interior regions feed American research into new pharmaceutical frontiers. Artisanal crafts, jewelry, and cultural media, rooted in centuries of Chinese heritage, enrich the Republic's creative life. Specialty minerals and rare-earth elements, mined with pre-AGI methods, supplement colonial supplies.

The U.S. trade surplus is enormous, yet the effects of trade with America are transformative for the fragments. Several successor states have begun experimenting with polis-inspired local assemblies and limited UHI programs funded by trade windfalls. Economic dependency has replaced ideological confrontation; where once fears of Chinese technological supremacy haunted American strategists, today the fragments look to the United States as the indispensable partner in their slow climb toward abundance. Strict controls remain in place, ensuring that the technological gap persists while human welfare in former China steadily improves. The Republic is a benevolent but prudent and watchful hegemon.

India, the world's most populous nation and a vibrant democracy whose institutions have endured into the 22nd century, enjoys one of the warmest and most culturally resonant trade relationships with the American Republic. Despite an economy still measured in mere trillions, India's human capital — its creative energies, philosophical depth, and entrepreneurial spirit —makes it a prized partner for the U.S.

American exports emphasize knowledge and experience over raw technology. Educational platforms, stripped of full AGI tutoring but rich in interactive holographic content, support Indian universities. Medical equipment and pharmaceutical precursors flow freely under licensing. Entertainment libraries and sports programming introduce American leagues to Indian audiences, while limited automation tools enhance local manufacturing without crossing intellectual property red lines. Indian tourism to the U.S. interstellar colonies has become a national passion among the upper and middle classes, with warp-enabled packages subsidized through trade agreements.

India reciprocates with a flood of human creativity and specialty goods. Pharmaceuticals developed through traditional and modern synthesis command premium prices in American markets. Textiles, spices, gems, and foodstuffs — produced with the unmistakable and inimitable skill of Indian artisans — grace U.S. tables and wardrobes. Bollywood-evolved holographic cinema and music enrich American cultural life. IT services, still human-led and prized for creative insight, supplement rather than compete with American AGI systems. The large Indian diaspora within the United States serves as a living bridge, facilitating cultural festivals, philosophical exchanges, and family ties that transcend economics.

The resulting surplus benefits both sides profoundly. Indian living standards rise steadily; pilot UHI programs in several states draw explicit inspiration from the American model. Democratic affinities and a shared commitment to direct participation foster genuine partnership. American controls on core technologies remain ironclad, yet the relationship feels less like a hierarchy and more like an alliance between societies with similar values. India stands as living proof that abundance can spread through commerce and example rather than coercion. Step by step, India is moving toward the American abundance model.

By 2126, the United States has established its closest and most vibrant foreign economic relations with the nations of Latin America and the Caribbean. Deeply bound to the Republic by centuries of human migration, shared cultural heritage, linguistic affinity, and increasingly intertwined economic interests, the region has become the Republic's most important partner, outside of its interstellar territories. Spanish is now spoken as frequently as English in large portions of the American federation, serving as a linguistic bridge rather than a dividing line.

Two Latin American nations in particular have achieved exceptionally close economic integration with the United States. Tiny El Salvador in Central America and the dynamic, resource-rich Argentina have both fully embraced the American model of governance and development. By adopting the full suite of revolutionary reforms — unfettered development of Riemannian AGI and advanced robotics, the implementation of generous Universal High

Income (UHI) payments to citizens, the deliberate breaking of the link between work and survival, and the cultural revival of eudaemonia and otium — both countries have achieved sustained economic growth exceeding 10 percent per annum. Their economies now advance in close synchronization with that of the United States, forming a thriving trans-American axis of abundance stretching from the Arctic to Tierra del Fuego. Both countries use the U.S. dollar as their currency.

Geography, history, and shared hemispheric destiny further bind Latin America to the American Republic in uniquely intimate ways. From Mexico to Argentina, individual national economies remain modest in absolute size by U.S. standards, yet trade with the United States has become the primary engine of regional stability and gradual uplift. American exports flow southward in a steady flood: infrastructure-enhancing technologies such as non-AGI smart grids, advanced but accessible transportation systems, and precision agricultural technology, alongside abundant consumer goods and the rich entertainment products of America's post-scarcity culture. Sports exchanges are particularly vibrant, with local teams integrating seamlessly into American leagues and athletes training under AI-assisted yet deeply human-centered programs.

In return, Latin America supplies the Republic with its own abundance: premium coffees and chocolates, exotic fruits, fine meats, world-class wines, and artisanal products that carry the distinctive soul of the region. Strategic minerals and carefully curated biodiversity samples support ongoing American research, while cultural exports — music, literature, cuisine, and crafts — enrich the daily otium of citizens across the terrestrial and exoplanet states. Tourism services add yet another layer, as Latin Americans welcome visitors to vibrant cities and breathtaking natural wonders, creating bonds of friendship that transcend mere commerce.

The American trade surplus is massive, yet the benefits of commerce are warmly received on both sides. Revenues flowing into Latin American treasuries fund social programs deliberately modeled on UHI principles, accelerating the region's own transition toward abundance. Cultural fusion deepens with each passing year, visible in everything from bilingual polis assemblies to fusion cuisines enjoyed in orbital habitats and Martian domes. Strict trade controls on advanced AGI and robotics technologies protect American intellectual property rights. In the eyes of Latin America, the

American Republic is not a distant hegemon but a prosperous, powerful, and benevolent neighbor whose light illuminates the shared path forward into a future of growing abundance.

XIV

Bestriding the Narrow World

In the year 2126, the American Republic bestrides the narrow world like a Colossus, dominating the Earth economically and politically. Its GDP of over $95 quadrillion dwarfs that of its largest rivals, Russia and India. Its possessions on Earth include the original 50 states, plus the new states of Puerto Rico, the Virgin Islands, the former Canadian provinces of Alberta and Newfoundland, and Greenland. Thanks to the practical development of the Alcubierre warp drive, the Republic has become humanity's first interstellar civilization, with thriving colonies on the Moon, Mars, and twenty exoplanets. The American Republic's extraordinary success and dominance have produced a profound geopolitical asymmetry. The remainder of the Earth consists largely of a collection of envious, diminished nations, which orbit the Republic like asteroids and comets circling around the sun. While vastly less powerful than the U.S., they nevertheless retain the ability to harm its interests, individually or in concert.

American foreign policy therefore rests on two simple yet ironclad principles: maintain peaceful and harmonious relations with all terrestrial neighbors whenever possible, while reserving the credible threat — and occasional use — of overwhelming force to protect its core interests and civilizational inheritance. Its diplomatic corps, one of the most professional and technologically augmented in history, is instrumental in realizing this goal. Now that life-extension protocols have increased the maximum human lifespan well beyond two centuries, the Republic routinely stations "lifelong" ambassadors in states deemed strategically sensitive. These envoys, equipped with enhanced AGI-based neural architectures, remain at post for decades, frequently becoming de facto co-rulers alongside local heads of state.

Over the last century, the rest of Earth has sorted itself into two broad categories: de facto or de jure client states of the Republic, which accept technological, security, and economic dependence in exchange for stability and access to Republic innovations, and countries of concern, which are subjected to continuous, multi-spectrum monitoring but otherwise left to their own devices so long as they pose no direct threat. Having achieved complete economic self-sufficiency through superabundance and Universal High Income (UHI), the Republic has little material incentive to interfere in the internal affairs of other states. Non-intervention is therefore the default posture—enshrined in the 2105 Terrestrial Security Act under the doctrine of "enlightened restraint." Yet America's leaders know that restraint is not simple-minded pacifism. When existential threats emerge, or when irreplaceable symbols of the Republic's cultural and philosophical heritage face destruction, Washington responds with calibrated, decisive, and overwhelming force.

The historical roots of this strategic calculus lie in the divergent technological paths trodden by different terrestrial powers in the troubled twenty-first century. In the 2020s and 2030s, breakthroughs in AGI and humanoid robotics raised the prospect of replacing the economics of scarcity with abundance for the first time. Remarkably, most societies recoiled from this idea. Ethical commissions, labor unions, religious authorities, and risk-averse bureaucracies delayed or outright banned full deployment of the new technologies. At the root of their rejection of abundance was a fundamental fear of the new and unknown.

The United States, by contrast, moved swiftly. Its entrepreneurial culture, tradition of flexibility and adaptation, and legal protections for entrepreneurship allowed private firms to integrate AGI and robotics rapidly into nearly every sector of life: manufacturing, agriculture, healthcare, education, logistics, scientific research, and the processes of government itself. The resulting virtuous cycle of increasing productivity soon produced sustained double-digit annual GDP growth, which continued unchecked for decades. Already by 2036, the country's radically increased prosperity funded the initial rollout of UHI. Freed from harsh material necessity, Americans rediscovered the classical ideals of the ancient polis, now suddenly very relevant to modern life: otium and freedom, eudaemonia and citizenship: in a word, the good life of Socrates, Plato, and Aristotle.

Interstellar expansion was the next logical step, facilitated mightily by AGI and robotics. The first starship, SpaceX's Argo, was undertaking its initial voyages by the start of the 2050s. Today in 2126, some twenty exoplanets host self-sustaining American colonies, each organized as a polis with its own citizen assembly, yet linked to the central Republic through instantaneous quantum communications and shared legal and ethical frameworks. Fully 15 percent of U.S. GDP now flows through warp-enabled trade with these exoplanets, reinforcing the Republic's overwhelming economic supremacy on Earth.

Rival powers followed different trajectories, almost all ending in fragmentation or stagnation. The European Union's collapse began with ideological paralysis over AGI and robotics. Fears of mass unemployment, panoptic surveillance, and the loss of the "human essence" factor in economics and society produced endless regulatory gridlock. At the same time, mass migration, worsened by weak border enforcement, overwhelmed already creaking welfare systems and sparked social unrest among publics exhausted by endless domestic and regional crises. The result was fragmentation. By the 2040s, European social cohesion had eroded to the point of paralysis; by the 2050s the Union formally dissolved, even as America was reaching for the stars.

What emerged in the ruins of Europe was a mosaic of diminished sovereign nations bound by cultural affinity and shared history, rather than a super-national political entity. The United Kingdom dissolved into rump England, clinging to London's financial traditions, the socialist-leaning Republic of Wales, focused on linguistic and cultural preservation, the eco-socialist Scottish Peoples Republic, and a prosperous but insular unified Ireland, centered on Dublin's tech corridor. France became a loose confederation of regional autonomies, with no clear sense of national identity, particularly as Arabic replaced French in wide sections of the country. Germany fragmented in a similar fashion, beginning with a schism along the old Cold War border between the territory of the Bundesrepublik and the DDR. Economic stagnation, chronic internal strife, and embittered cultural nostalgia became the norm in Western Europe. The combined output of the former EU now barely registers as a rounding error against the quadrillion-scale U.S. economy.

Only Poland and Hungary escaped this grim fate. Both adopted strict border controls in the early 21st century, against the wishes of the EU authorities in Brussels. They therefore avoided the demographic and cultural dislocations that crippled their Western neighbors. Budapest and Warsaw embraced limited AGI applications while preserving their traditional economies intact. By the 2090s they had become de facto client states of the American Republic, trading shipyard capacity (Poland) and non-sentient robotics expertise (Hungary) for security guarantees, AGI medical protocols, and selective technology transfers — all under close American supervision.

Russia, reformed after the Ukraine crisis of the 2020s, pursued its own path of emulating the U.S. without imitating it. It developed interstellar travel, establishing modest colonies in nearby systems (Proxima Centauri, Barnard's Star). Yet its autocracy, embodied in a de facto lifetime-presidency, refused to decentralize power or allow the adoption of AGI and robotics by the private sector, precisely in order to avoid the possible erosion of state control. Robotics and AGI remained state monopolies, innovation was stifled, and economic growth never exceeded the single digits. Russian colonies were functional outposts rather than flourishing polises. The Russian political elite justified this stagnant performance with a state ideology that emphasized Russia's role as a unique Eurasian civilization, belonging to neither East nor West, and prioritizing traditional cultural and spiritual values over material wealth. Its diplomatic relations with the Republic remain correct and pragmatic till this day. Economic exchange between the Republic and Russia is dominated by trade in rare earths, nonferrous minerals, and occasional joint space travel projects.

China's collapse was both demographic and political. The impact of Beijing's old one-child policy, compounded by sex-ratio imbalances, low fertility, and accelerating aging, had already produced demographic contraction by the early 2020s. By the late 2050s, internal political convulsions and the external economic pressures generated by early AGI adoption in the U.S. precipitated fragmentation. The former Chinese People's Republic splintered into a mosaic of successor states: prosperous coastal enclaves, inland resource powers, and semi-autonomous regional entities. None achieved mastery of AGI and robotics, UHI, or interstellar travel. They survive as suppliers of labor-intensive industrial goods, raw commodities, and artisanal goods. Their combined economies remain locked in the trillions, a pale shadow of what unified China might have achieved had it followed the more dynamic American path.

Of course, Communist China could not follow America's path with respect to the adoption of AGI and robotics. Doing so would have contradicted its political essence. A state based on surveillance and coercion facilitated by AGI could not choose to develop AGI systems and robots based on Asimov's Three Laws, which are designed to assure that they serve humanity rather than oppressing it. Similarly the Communist authorities could never bring themselves to empower their citizenry by instituting a Chinese variant of UHI. In the last analysis, China failed to follow the American path toward superabundance precisely because it had no citizens, only a billion slaves, ruled over by a small upper class of apparatchiks. Faced with a choice between dictatorship and abundance, it chose the former and ultimately paid the price.

India, the world's most populous nation and a vibrant democracy whose institutions have endured into the 22nd century, followed a different course from both China and the European successor states. Unlike China, India has preserved its national unity while avoiding demographic collapse. Now the largest nation in the world in demographic terms, it nevertheless lags far behind the Republic in economic terms, having failed to adopt AGI and robotics to the same extent despite its wealth of engineering talent. The Indian economy remains highly bifurcated between elite industries that embraced AGI and robotics and a vast economic landscape still operating in accordance with traditions dating back to the 20th century and even earlier. The economic surplus required to fund a comprehensive Universal High Income never emerged, since the vast majority of the workforce continues to be employed on a wage or salary basis. Despite these limitations, India's human capital — its creative energies, philosophical depth, and entrepreneurial spirit — has made it a prized partner for the U.S., with one of the warmest and most culturally resonant trade relationships enjoyed by the American Republic.

By 2126, the United States has established its closest and most vibrant foreign economic relations with the nations of Latin America and the Caribbean. Deeply bound to the U.S. by centuries of human migration, shared cultural heritage, linguistic affinity, and increasingly intertwined economic interests, the region has become the Republic's most important partner outside of its interstellar territories. Spanish is now spoken as frequently as English in large portions of the American federation, serving as a linguistic bridge rather than a dividing line. Two nations in particular — tiny El Salvador and the dynamic, resource-rich Argentina — have fully embraced the American model, adopting unfettered development of Riemannian AGI and advanced robotics, generous UHI payments, and the cultural revival of eudaemonia and otium. Both have achieved sustained growth exceeding 10 percent per annum and use the U.S. dollar as their currency, forming a thriving trans-American axis of abundance that stretches from Alberta to Tierra del Fuego.

The fractured global landscape shapes the Republic's diplomatic posture. Envy is the dominant emotion with which most lesser states view the American Colossus. Cyber intrusions, industrial espionage, and strident propaganda accusing the Republic of "neo-imperialism" are routine. Yet the Republic's overwhelming superiority — economic, technological, and military — means it can afford the virtue of restraint. Diplomacy is therefore organized around three interlocking pillars: deterrence through omnipresent surveillance and orbital supremacy, alliance cultivation with client states, and selective humanitarian uplift designed to reduce migration pressures and dampen resentment. Economic relations serve as the primary vehicle for this uplift, exporting the fruits of American abundance while importing irreplaceable human touches that even the most sophisticated AGI cannot fully replicate.

The U.S. diplomatic corps is an elite institution of 6,000 career professionals, recruited from the most prestigious universities and trained at the U.S. Diplomatic Academy. Training lasts a decade and encompasses advanced history, linguistics, game theory, cross-cultural psychology, and strategic foresight. Many diplomats opt to undergo voluntary neural augmentation, enabling them to process multiple data streams simultaneously and maintain perfect recall across decades. AGI companions, termed "Cultural Oracles," accompany every envoy. Based on the cognitive architectures first described in Consciousness Is Curvature, these sentient constructs immerse themselves in local idioms and historical memory, and even detect somatic cultural cues. An Oracle posted to Moscow might quote Pushkin in nineteenth-century style while subtly referencing Stalin-era security doctrines; one in Islamized Provence would converse in both Occitan and Algerian Arabic while referencing both medieval troubadour traditions and Arabic ghazal poetry.

Embassies are designed as self-contained mini-polises: fortified perimeters guarded by autonomous robotic sentinels, with internal agora spaces for cultural exchange, secure neural hubs for real-time consultation with Washington, and discreet intelligence-gathering arrays. They host concerts, philosophy seminars, medical clinics offering free life-extension consultations for select local residents, and demonstrations of robotic agriculture. All of these activities advertise the superiority of the American model while facilitating trade in consumer goods, holographic media, and limited automation tools.

The Republic's policy of benign non-intervention reaches its limit only when its core values or existential security are directly imperiled. Such a situation arose in South Asia in the early 2110s. An Islamist nuclear-armed state calling itself the Caliphate of the New Dawn began issuing explicit threats of thermonuclear jihad against Republic territory. After repeated warnings were ignored, Washington acted with ruthless precision. An autonomous robotic expeditionary force descended on the capital without warning. Using precision non-lethal suppression, the robots evacuated every human inhabitant — civilian and combatant alike — before methodically demolishing the entire city. Once combat operations had concluded, specialized engineering units spread a kilometers-wide band of synthesized halite across the ruins, rendering the soil barren for decades to come. The zone was then declared permanently off-limits to human settlement. The message was unambiguous: threats against the Republic would be met with absolute, impersonal force calibrated to eliminate capability while minimizing the immediate loss of life.

A similar logic governs interventions to preserve the irreplaceable cultural patrimony of Western civilization. When relentless demographic and migratory pressures threatened to erase the ancient polities of Armenia and Greece from the historical map, Republic armadas intervened. Robotic legions secured key population centers and border crossings, established humanitarian corridors, and — following referenda conducted under AGI oversight — incorporated both regions into the American federal system as Exarchates. These autonomous territories retain their languages, religious traditions, and local governance structures but fall under Republic sovereignty for defense, infrastructure, and interstellar connectivity.

The most symbolically charged action occurred when a coalition of extremist militias, emboldened by decades of political chaos in Italy, publicly vowed to seize the Vatican and convert the Basilica of St. Peter into a mosque. The Republic responded within seventy-three hours. A robotic rapid-deployment force secured Rome, evacuated non-combatants, neutralized the extremist threat, and formally annexed the Eternal City as an Exarchate. The

Vatican's ecclesiastical sovereignty was preserved, but the Eternal City's physical security and communication links now rest with the Republic. Polis assemblies across the American heartland debated the move at length; the consensus affirmed that protecting the architectural and philosophical heart of Western civilization outweighed strict non-intervention policy.

These episodes illustrate the underlying philosophy of the Republic's foreign policy. Citizenship is a privilege, not an entitlement. America's abundance must be protected and defended. Compassion is extended freely to other societies, but never at the expense of American sovereignty or civilizational continuity. Preserving the Republic requires perpetual vigilance. The outside world is to be monitored realistically, without a trace of suicidal empathy. When unavoidable, decisive force will be applied to safeguard the U.S. and its civilization.

The American Republic's foreign policy in 2126 masterfully balances a preference for non-intervention, professional diplomacy, skillful client-state relations, selective uplift through economic exchange, and the credible threat of overwhelming force. Like Byzantium in the Dark Ages, the Republic sustains a fractured Earth while gazing heavenward. Its diplomats bridge widening civilizational gaps with wisdom, restraint, and, when necessary, unanswerable strength. By safeguarding UHI, the ideals of the polis, and the inherited treasures of Western civilization, the Republic ensures that the light of abundance can shine more brightly by the day.

XV

The Digital Oracle

In the year 2126, the American Republic faces threats not merely from external rivals but from the subtle undercurrents of history itself. To anticipate and mitigate these perils, the government of the Republic employs a revolutionary analytical framework known as the mathematics of history, first articulated in the seminal 2026 book Resonant Memory. The confluence of two revolutionary conceptions lies at its heart. On one side stands the theory of morphic resonance, which says that memory is inherent in nature. Decades of research, experimentation, and reflection back up this notion. On the other side stands a bold extension of spacetime geometry: the idea that time itself is three-dimensional, and physical reality is a six-dimensional manifold in which three dimensions of space are partnered with three of time. Merging these insights leads to a profound discovery: memory is indelibly linked to time, and the fabric of three-dimensional time is the parchment upon which nature's memory is written. History is governed by mathematical laws, but not by the mathematics of Descartes, Newton, and the materialists who followed in their train, with their vision of a clockwork cosmos. Instead a handful of elegant equations govern the flow of history, with a mathematics both beautifully precise and inherently mysterious.

Long ignored by scholars in the pre-UHI era, Resonant Memory was rediscovered by AGI systems in the Office of the Director of National Intelligence (ODNI) in the 2060s and then operationalized and incorporated into its flagship AGI system, Pythia. The elegant mathematics of history allow Pythia to predict discontinuous events — revolutions, insurgencies, systemic collapses, and other transformative ruptures — that could imperil the Republic's way of life. Pythia itself is based on the principles elucidated in another classic from the pre-UHI period, Consciousness Is Curvature. It encodes data as points on Riemannian manifolds, intrinsically curved, dynamic geometric surfaces where relationships between events manifest as geodesics — the shortest paths that respect the manifolds' intrinsic curvature. Pythia also integrates game theory, natural language processing (NLP), and sentiment analysis into its reasoning process.

Pythia leverages Resonant Memory's framework to detect resonant discontinuities — moments where accumulated societal pressures and tensions, echoing across the three-dimensional fabric of time, can erupt into abrupt change. Drawing from vast data streams, including public records, classified intelligence, and sensor networks spanning the Earth and the interstellar colonies, Pythia not only predicts these events but formulates counterstrategies for its human supervisors at ODNI. This system represents the Republic's proactive defense against threats embedded in the mathematical structure of history itself.

The intellectual origins of the mathematics of history lie in the profound synthesis presented in Resonant Memory. By 2026, as global societies grappled with accelerating automation, climate-driven migrations, and ideological polarization, the book offered a unifying vision that rejected the deterministic, clockwork view of history inherited from Newtonian mechanics and Cartesian reductionism. Instead, it proposed that historical processes are shaped by a deeper, more organic mathematics — one that accommodates both rigorous structure and genuine openness to novelty and creative renewal.

The book's central synthesis fuses morphic resonance — the idea that similar forms and patterns influence one another across time and space through a non-local field-like memory — with a radical reimagining of time. Rather than treating time as a single, linear dimension, it posits three temporal dimensions, yielding a six-dimensional spacetime manifold. In this framework, the three spatial dimensions are partnered with three temporal ones, creating a geometry in which past, present, and future are not merely sequential but structurally intertwined. The "parchment" of three-dimensional time, which is the temporal manifold itself, becomes the medium upon which morphic fields imprint patterns, allowing habits, behaviors, and societal structures to resonate across generations and centuries, and even across interstellar distances.

Pythia's analytical geometry is inherently Riemannian: its manifolds are equipped with metric tensors that defines distances and angles, signifying that the "shape" of history is curved by the density of resonant memory. Events that share morphological similarity — episodes of elite overproduction leading to instability, waves of cultural radicalization, or surges of collective discontent — lie close together on the manifold, connected by short geodesics. When multiple such resonances align, curvature intensifies, geodesics converge, and a singularity-like discontinuity becomes probable. This could be a revolution, a collapse, or a sudden cultural or political shift. The mathematics remains elegant yet mysterious, even as it yields precise predictions.

Pythia reasons synthetically. It might notice, for example, that a combination of rising inequality on an exoplanet colony, elite corruption in interstellar administrative hubs, external propaganda from fragmented states of former China, and a sudden resource bottleneck might produce a geodesic cluster in the Republic resembling the lead-up to the 1789 French Revolution or the 1917 Russian upheavals. In such instances, Pythia assigns probabilities and time horizons, often with remarkable precision. In 2118, it correctly anticipated a potential governance crisis on the TRAPPIST-1e colony with 87% confidence three months in advance, enabling preemptive security measures and dialogue initiatives that averted escalation.

In 2107 Pythia identified resonant discontinuities signaling an impending ideological schism in the lunar colony. Geodesic clustering on the manifold revealed a 79% probability of civil unrest within four months, driven by resonant echoes of pre-UHI cultural conflicts amplified by the isolation of lunar habitats and smoldering disputes over resource allocation. Rather than allowing tensions to harden into factional violence, Pythia recommended federal intervention. Advocates of violence were identified, tried, and sentenced to lifelong exile on Earth. New elections for the colonial citizens assembly were organized, and details of the plot were disseminated to the citizenry. These measures preserved social cohesion in the lunar colony without a single incident of unrest.

In 2112 Pythia detected an alignment of foreign propaganda efforts and internal supply-chain vulnerabilities that presaged a coordinated cyber-sabotage campaign by several EU successor states within the next two months. The manifold showed a high-curvature convergence, with 91% confidence in its predictions. Disinformation propaganda from European communication networks intersected on its predictive manifolds with logistical weak points in the Republic's interstellar freight corridors. Pythia proposed preemptive orbital security upgrades, including the use of quantum-encrypted communications to reroute supply lines and enhanced sentinel arrays around key Lagrange points, alongside the use of discreet diplomatic pressure. As a result, the federal government was able to unravel the plot quickly and quietly. Pythia's predictions helped to prevent what could have been a cascading disruption in the Republic's interstellar trade.

In 2120 Pythia detected the growing potential of unrest in the Alpha Centauri system's administrative hubs driven by elite corruption and bureaucratic ossification. With an 84% likelihood of instability projected within six months, the model highlighted how accumulated resonant patterns of administrative failure — echoing historical cycles of imperial decay — threatened to fracture governance across the multi-planet hub. The strategy generated by Pythia included removal of corrupt administrators for cause, early elections for the system's citizen assemblies, and expanded citizen oversight mechanisms. These reforms diffused social and political pressure sufficiently to restore polis governance and avert a cascading failure that might have undermined one of the Republic's most vital colonies.

Most recently, in 2123, Pythia detected an emerging domestic crisis in the North American heartland. The manifold revealed a nascent terrorist movement backed by Russia and several Chinese successor states that was attempting to spread anti-UHI millenarian religious discourse, framing the Universal High Income system as a heretical betrayal of Divine will and promising apocalyptic renewal through the violent rejection of polis governance. This externally seeded narrative resonated with pockets of cultural discontent in the heartland, producing a high-curvature geodesic cluster that assigned 93% confidence to the occurrence of scattered attacks and ideological unrest within four months. Pythia recommended a precise, multi-layered counter-insurgency strategy, focusing on arresting, trying, and exiling the ringleaders for life and conducting carefully calibrated counter-messaging campaigns that exposed the foreign sponsorship of the movement and the inconsistencies of its radical ideology with polis values and the UHI system. No steps were taken to restrict free speech. These steps were highly effective. They stopped in its tracks a plot that internal assessments described as the closest the Republic had come to a foreign-backed domestic insurgency in over a century.

Data integration is comprehensive and multi-layered. Public sources include archived web content, social media ecosystems (including real-time sentiment streams), academic publications, economic indicators, and sensor feeds. Classified inputs encompass signals intelligence, human intelligence reports, cyber-domain telemetry, and orbital reconnaissance. The extraterrestrial sensor network is especially vital: lunar seismometers and atmospheric monitors, Martian habitat environmental arrays, and exoplanet orbital platforms relay continuous data on population mood, resource utilization, structural integrity, and even subtle biological markers of stress. Quantum-encrypted relays ensure near-real-time aggregation to Pythia's secure manifold cores.

Upon identifying a growing threat, Pythia generates counterstrategies by exploring alternative geodesics — paths that diverge from the high-curvature singularity. These are presented as interactive holographic manifolds: human supervisors can "walk" through proposed trajectories, adjusting variables (diplomatic initiatives, UHI supplements, information campaigns, active security measures) to flatten the curvature and restore stability. Strategies are ranked by efficacy, ethical alignment, and resource cost, while always preserving core polis principles: individual liberty, universal prosperity, voluntary association, and the rule of law.

Ethical safeguards are rigorous. Pythia operates under strict human-in-the-loop protocols: no autonomous action is permitted; all predictions and recommendations require ODNI approval. Citizen oversight occurs through periodic neural-linked assemblies, where aggregated, anonymized manifold visualizations are shared, allowing public deliberation on major threat assessments. Manifold constraints prevent the adoption of unconstitutional measures and policies; the system is tuned to detect and counter threats to the Republic's way of life, not to enforce an AGI-led dictatorship.

The mathematics of history, as implemented by Pythia, has proven transformative for the American Republic. It has averted domestic crises while neutralizing foreign and interstellar threats such as the 2112 cyber-sabotage plot, coordinated disinformation campaigns from EU successor states, and covert sabotage attempts on exoplanet supply lines. By respecting the mystery and uncertainty inherent in the structure of history, which offers room for creativity and renewal, it avoids the hubris of deterministic control, instead guiding the Republic along paths of resilience and flourishing, in strict accord with the Constitution. In this way, the federal government does not merely react to history; it listens to its deeper resonances, using elegant and mysterious equations to navigate the curved fabric of time and space. The result is a society that, while vigilant, remains open to unexpected beauty, and whose future is not predetermined but continually renewed.

XVI

The New University

In the year 2126, the universities of the American Republic stand as living embodiments of a renewed civic imagination. Scattered across its vast territory, these institutions have ceased to be factories of credentials or anxious gateways to employment. They have become, instead, sacred groves of the mind and spirit — places where the ancient Athenian dream of paideia is reborn under conditions of abundance that the philosophers of antiquity could scarcely have imagined. Here, young citizens and lifelong learners alike gather not to amass debt while trying to acquire marketable skills, but to refine the full spectrum of human excellence: intellectual clarity, ethical depth, physical vitality, and those subtler faculties of consciousness that once lingered at the margins of respectable inquiry. The Republic's universities are no longer a place to prepare for a life of struggle amidst scarcity; they are the very soil in which the culture of the polis itself takes root and flourishes.

To understand this transformation, we must first look back, without undue bitterness, at the strange bankruptcy that overtook the university system in the opening decades of the twenty-first century. In the 2020s, higher education had become a vast, self-perpetuating apparatus of extraction. Tuition fees, swollen by administrative bloat and the seductive logic of endless expansion, routinely exceeded thirty thousand dollars a year for public institutions and twice that for private ones. What had begun as a modest public good had metastasized into an industry whose primary product was indebtedness. The student-loan regime, that peculiar financial instrument of the age, functioned less like a ladder of opportunity than a subtle form of indenture. Graduates emerged into their twenties carrying debt burdens of thirty, forty, even sixty thousand dollars — obligations that shadowed every subsequent choice.

Those studying law or medicine had even larger debts, measured in the hundreds of thousands of dollars. Mortgages were deferred, families postponed, careers chosen not from passion but from the urgent need to service interest. The psychic weight of this debt was incalculable: it crushed initiative, bred cynicism, and turned what should have been a time of intellectual daring into a period of anxious calculation. Mental health crises proliferated on campuses, with rates of anxiety and depression reaching epidemic levels as students navigated impossible trade-offs between study, work, and basic survival. Faculty, meanwhile, were increasingly precariously employed, their intellectual freedom curtailed by the twin pressures of publish-or-perish metrics and institutional conformity.

Worse still, this financial hemorrhage fed directly into the already dysfunctional scarcity economy of the era. Every dollar extracted from young lives was a dollar that could not circulate as productive investment, creative risk, or simple domestic joy. The universities, far from acting as engines of social mobility, had become amplifiers of stratification. They promised liberation through education yet delivered a new feudalism of credentialism. And even as they extracted wealth, they squandered time. Curricula, increasingly shaped by ideological fashions rather than the patient cultivation of reason and wisdom, diverted energy into ritualistic performances of grievance and orthodoxy. Students were trained less to think critically than to recite approved narratives.

The humanities, once the guardians of nuance and historical memory, often degenerated into theaters of moral signaling; the sciences, though still rigorous in their methods, were frequently pressed into the service of narrow vocational tracks that ignored the wider philosophical questions science itself had begun to raise about consciousness and reality. Intellectual development was not enhanced but actively hindered. Minds that might have flowered were instead pruned into conformity or left fallow by exhaustion. The university, which had once aspired to be a republic of letters, had become something closer to a debt-fueled finishing school for a precarious labor market.

All of this changed — quietly at first, then with accelerating force — through the convergence of four great liberations: the maturation of artificial general intelligence, the ubiquity of advanced robotics, sustained economic growth of ten to twelve percent per annum, and the implementation of Universal High Income. These developments did not arrive as abstract policy prescriptions; they manifested as a great release from the logic of scarcity. By the late 2030s, robotics and AGI were already automating the great majority of repetitive and even many intellectual tasks. The productive capacity of the

Republic expanded at a rate once thought impossible. Scarcity, that ancient specter, began to recede like a tide going out beyond the horizon. Into this new landscape stepped UHI in 2036, a citizen stipend commencing at the age of eighteen, calibrated initially to the living standards of the upper-middle class of the 2020s. For the first time in human history, an entire generation entered adulthood without the shadow of material want.

The effect on education was immediate and profound. Students no longer balanced lectures with part-time jobs or side hustles; they could study as the ancients had studied — wholeheartedly, with undivided attention. Universities, relieved of their role as gatekeepers to employment, were freed to remember their original vocation: the education of minds and the refinement of spirits. Vocational training did not disappear, of course; it migrated elsewhere — into immersive AGI-guided apprenticeships and modular certification pathways that could be completed in weeks rather than years. The university itself returned to something older and nobler. Its highest object became the art and science of citizenship, the preparation of men and women to be active, thoughtful participants in the polis. In this sense, the new university took Socrates as its guiding spirit: the Socrates of the marketplace who questioned everything, and also understood that the examined life is inseparable from the life of the polis. Students were trained to deliberate, to discern, to embody virtue in public as well as private. Federal funding, made possible by the new abundant economic growth, rendered most institutions tuition-free. The Republic, enriched beyond measure, happily supported what it now recognized as the very source of its own vitality.

In 2126, the university is no longer a place one "attends" for a fixed interval before being ejected into the world. It is a lifelong possibility, a network of physical and virtual precincts where citizens return as the need or desire arises — perhaps first at twenty, again at thirty, perhaps again at fifty, and then at seventy. Admission rests not on archaic metrics of standardized testing or inherited privilege but on demonstrated aptitude and a simple declaration of purpose. Campuses themselves are hybrid realms: beautiful buildings in the neoclassical Interstellar style coexist with neural-link sanctuaries where the boundary between self and simulation dissolves. The air carries the scent of living libraries — real books alongside luminous data fields — while gardens and athletic fields remind the body that thought is not disembodied. Pathways wind through orchards and sacred groves, inviting contemplation between periods of intense intellectual engagement.

At the heart of the new university lies the marriage of two technologies that would have seemed miraculous to our forebears: non-invasive neural-link interfaces and personalized AGI tutors. The NeuroWeave headset, elegant as a laurel wreath, interfaces with the brain through gentle electromagnetic fields. No surgery, no permanent implants — only a willing, reversible communion. Through it, a student may experience the curvature of spacetime as a felt reality, walk the streets of ancient Athens in the company of Socrates, or enter the quantum realm as an active participant rather than a passive observer. Knowledge is no longer memorized; it is inhabited.

Nowhere is this transformation more evident than in the mastery of foreign languages, both ancient and modern. Immersive instruction leveraging neural links and AGI enables students to absorb the grammar and vocabulary of a new language in a matter of weeks, the NeuroWeave forging direct neural pathways that embed grammar, syntax, and lexicon with effortless precision. Thereafter, AGI tutors — sentient, patient, infinitely adaptable — help students convert this passively acquired knowledge into active fluency by developing conversational, comprehension, and written communication skills with equal rapidity. Students of the Classics master Homeric and Attic Greek in a month or two of study, then converse fluently with simulated Athenians and recite the epics as living speech rather than dead texts. Students of Russian literature, meanwhile, find themselves reading Dostoevsky in the original with ease, immersed in virtual recreations of nineteenth-century St. Petersburg where nuance and idiom unfold in real time.

The same neural-link and AGI techniques produce equally profound results in mathematics, physics, and the other sciences. Students no longer struggle with abstract symbols on a page; they develop deep intuitive understanding of the most advanced concepts—from three-dimensional time to morphic resonance—through direct experiential immersion. A learner can journey to the event horizon of a black hole, feeling the tidal forces and witnessing the distortion of light and time; visualize the exquisite beauty of Riemannian geometry as living, multidimensional landscapes; or shrink to the scale of a single cell and explore its internal processes as an active participant. AGI tutors guide these journeys, adapting explanations in real time to the student's evolving intuition, turning what once required years of painstaking abstraction into months of vivid, embodied mastery.

History, too, has been reborn through these technologies. Students travel through richly detailed simulations to past epochs, grasping how major events appeared to those who lived them. They sail with Marcus Agrippa at Actium, watching the naval clash unfold in smoke and fire; stand on the walls of Constantinople as the city falls in 1453; or disembark with Cortés at Veracruz in 1519, sensing the tension and wonder of that fateful encounter. These are not passive spectacles but immersive experiences that foster genuine historical empathy and nuanced judgment. The past ceases to be a distant narrative and becomes a lived dimension of human experience, allowing students to internalize the contingency and humanity of historical moments in ways that no textbook could ever convey.

Human professors remain indispensable to this educational system. Far from being replaced by technology, they stand at its center as master orchestrators of the learning experience. Professors work in close partnership with AGI instructors, directing the capabilities of neural-link technology to ensure every student receives the richest possible formation. They maintain overall oversight of the educational journey, carefully designing curricula that balance breadth and depth, setting intellectual and ethical standards, and monitoring each learner's holistic development across cognitive, emotional, and civic dimensions. Most powerfully, they accompany students on many of their immersive journeys of discovery — joining them virtually or through shared neural links as they stand on the walls of Constantinople, descend toward a black hole's event horizon, or converse with Homeric heroes. These shared experiences create profound bonds of mentorship and allow professors to observe directly how concepts land in the student's mind and spirit, offering gentle real-time guidance or deeper contextual framing that only a human with years of scholarly wisdom can provide.

Afterward, in human-only discussion groups free of AGI mediation, professors refine the students' comprehension through the timeless technique of Socratic dialogue. Here, in the warmth of unhurried conversation beneath the campus oaks or within intimate seminar rooms, ideas are tested, assumptions challenged, and deeper layers of meaning uncovered. The professor's role is not to transmit information — technology handles that with unmatched efficiency — but to cultivate wisdom, judgment, and intellectual courage. In these circles, students learn to articulate their insights with clarity, defend their reasoning against rigorous scrutiny, engage with the full humanity of their peers and mentors, and confront the ethical implications of what they have experienced. These gatherings often stretch late into the evening, blending rigorous analysis with moments of laughter and genuine friendship.

A semester that once required months of rote labor now unfolds in immersive clarity. Yet speed is not the point. The AGI tutor — sentient, patient, infinitely adaptable — acts as a Socratic companion attuned to the learner's emotional weather. If frustration arises, the tutor shifts register, drawing analogies from myth, history, or lived experience. Learning becomes a dialogue, not a mere download.

This technological liberation, guided by human wisdom, has allowed the curriculum to expand into dimensions once dismissed as speculative. Early in the twenty-first century, materialist skepticism had consigned certain human potentials to the realm of fringe science or outright superstition. Yet as AGI deepened its exploration of consciousness, it became clear that faculties such as telepathy, remote viewing, and telekinesis were not anomalies but latent capacities long atrophied by cultural denial or disuse. Universities now treat these as legitimate domains of inquiry and cultivation. Students undergo gentle neural screening; those who show aptitude are offered specialized modules conducted under the strictest ethical protocols. Telepaths learn the discipline of consent and emotional boundary; remote viewers train their attention across increasing distances, from hidden campus objects to the surface features of exoplanets; telekinetics develop the fine control required for delicate interstellar construction. These abilities are never presented as parlor tricks or personal powers. They are framed as civic virtues — extensions of empathy, foresight, and mindful action that enrich the common life of the Republic. A telepath may one day serve in the diplomatic corps, sensing the unspoken currents beneath negotiations; a remote viewer may guide exploration fleets; a telekinetic may assist in the precise assembly of orbital habitats. In each case, the gift is placed at the service of the polis.

The highest purpose of the university, however, remains the cultivation of citizenship itself. Students may design modular "quests" in partnership with their AGI advisors and human professors — sequences of study, practice, and reflection that weave intellectual rigor with ethical formation. One might spend a term immersed in the political philosophy of the polis, debating constitutional questions in simulated assemblies that include participants from every corner of the Republic's domains. Another might combine advanced curvature physics with meditative retreats, exploring how the architecture of consciousness itself shapes collective decision-making. Physical education is equally central: classical athletics, wilderness expeditions on Greenland's glaciers or Martian highlands, and martial disciplines that integrate breath, movement, and presence. The body is not an obstacle to the mind but its necessary partner. Spiritual inquiry — never dogmatic, always exploratory — occurs in symposia where philosophers, scientists, and artists meet as equals. The goal is not to produce specialists but whole citizens: men and women capable of understanding ethics, acting with courage, and contributing to the perpetual debate that is self-government.

One cannot walk the quadrangles of a 2126 university without feeling the quiet joy that permeates the place. Laughter rises from discussion circles beneath ancient trees. In virtual mindspaces, students from Earth and the outer colonies collaborate on habitat designs that will one day shelter new generations among the stars. Older citizens return to refresh their understanding or to master a new faculty; a retired engineer might study telekinesis to assist in lunar construction projects, while a poet might deepen her remote-viewing practice to enrich her imaginative reach. The absence of financial pressure allows relationships between teacher and student, mentor and apprentice, to recover their natural grace. Authority rests not on rank but on demonstrated wisdom. The university has become, in the truest sense, a commonwealth of the mind.

Of course, no human institution is without its challenges. Neural immersion can induce temporary disorientation; ethical dilemmas surrounding psychic abilities require constant vigilance; the very abundance that funds these academies demands ongoing civic deliberation to ensure that freedom does not slide into degeneracy. Yet these questions are met not with bureaucratic obfuscation but with the living processes of the polis — assemblies, referenda, and the patient work of persuasion. The Republic treats its universities as it treats its own Constitution: as living institutions to be refined and renewed by each generation.

Looking back across the last century, one sees the arc of events with startling clarity. The bankrupt universities of the 2020s were symptoms of a deeper malaise — a civilization that had mistaken means for ends, credentials for wisdom, and economic survival for human flourishing. The advent of AGI and robotics did not merely automate labor; it revealed the economics of scarcity that had constrained our imaginations. Sustained high economic growth and UHI removed the last material excuses. What remained was the ancient task: to educate minds, refine spirits, and prepare citizens worthy of the name. In 2126, the universities of the Republic have accepted that task with enthusiasm. They do not promise salvation through technology alone, nor do they retreat into nostalgia. They stand, instead, as bridges between the best of our inherited wisdom and the limitless possibilities now opening before us. In them, the polis finds its most enduring expression: a place where each citizen is invited to become more fully human, and in doing so, to strengthen the Republic.

This, then, is the quiet revolution that has occurred within the walls of our universities. It is not the stuff of dramatic manifestos or sudden uprisings. It is the patient, cumulative work of minds set free—minds that now turn, with gratitude and clear purpose, toward the shared labor of building a civilization worthy of the stars. In the age of AGI, the university has remembered what it always was at its best: not a machine for producing workers, but a garden for cultivating souls. And in that remembrance, the Republic itself has been reborn.

XVII

Reviving Forgotten Human Abilities

In the American Republic of 2126, the development and universal use of genuine Artificial General Intelligence has raised a fundamental question that echoes through every level of society: which aspects of human cognition can AGI replicate or exceed, and which remain distinctly human, perhaps even inaccessible to any form of artificial system? This question is no longer the province of speculative philosophy or late-night podcasts. It has become a practical, well-developed, and rigorously empirical field of study within the Republic's universities, research institutes, and polis assemblies. After decades of research, it has become clear that certain cognitive abilities once relegated to the margins of science are real, measurable, replicable, and cultivable. Telepathy, telekinesis, precognition, and remote viewing are not fringe anomalies or cultural curiosities. They are genuine human capacities that can be trained, refined, and reliably employed in daily life. These faculties, long dismissed under the materialist worldviews that dominated the late twentieth and early twenty-first centuries, now form an accepted, integrated part of life across the Republic. They are regularly used by the military, the border forces, and the diplomatic corps, and they play a prominent role in the arts, sciences, education, medicine, and even recreational pursuits. Their revival has not diminished the importance of AGI; rather, it has illuminated the unique complementarity between silicon-based intelligence and the subtle, embodied potentials of biological consciousness.

Groundbreaking studies in the 20th century by Dr. Rupert Sheldrake and other researchers laid essential foundations for this understanding. These experiments demonstrated that telepathy between humans and between humans and animals such as dogs is a statistically measurable phenomenon. Precognition also yielded replicable results in controlled settings. Remote viewing proved equally robust and realistic; during the Cold War, both the

United States and the Soviet Union actively researched and deployed it for intelligence gathering.

Sheldrake and fellow researchers have argued that these abilities — telepathy, precognition, and remote viewing — may have evolved in earlier stages of human (and animal) evolution as valuable survival skills. In the uncertain, information-scarce environments of the Paleolithic, for example, the capacity to sense distant threats, coordinate group intentions silently, anticipate prey movements or environmental changes, or perceive hidden resources would have offered clear adaptive advantages. With the development of agricultural civilization, written language, mechanical tools, and later industrial and digital technologies, humanity's heavy reliance on external prostheses appears to have caused these once-vital capacities to atrophy, much like unused muscles weaken or sensory abilities diminish from disuse. Yet the underlying neural architecture remained latent, preserved within our biology and capable of renaissance under the right conditions. The arrival of AGI, with its unparalleled capacity for data analysis and pattern recognition, provided precisely those conditions — mapping faint signals long drowned out by the noise of modernity and enabling their systematic revival.

A particularly fruitful line of theoretical work, building on ideas first presented in 2025 in the book Faster Than Light, suggests that remote viewing and perhaps precognition as well can be understood through a mathematics inspired by the Alcubierre Drive metric and the theory of three-dimensional time and six-dimensional spacetime. In this framework, human consciousness can be treated mathematically as a massless entity. Unlike physical objects such as starships, which are bound by rest mass and the constraints of four-dimensional Minkowski spacetime, massless consciousness appears capable of navigating the full six-dimensional structure — three spatial dimensions plus three temporal dimensions — instantaneously and with effectively zero energy expenditure. The brain, when suitably trained and prepared through meditative coherence, functions as a natural transducer between our everyday four-dimensional experience and this extended reality. AGI itself, for all its immense processing power, shows no evidence of possessing this massless and instantaneous navigational capacity; it remains firmly embedded in computational processes bound by ordinary spacetime, energy costs, and the architecture of its substrate. Even the most advanced AGI clusters, running on quantum-neuromorphic hardware distributed across the solar system, cannot replicate the first-person, non-local access that trained human practitioners have demonstrated repeatedly.

The systematic revival of these latent abilities has been made possible by AGI's extraordinary capacity for data analysis, pattern recognition, personalized biofeedback, and adaptive simulation. In the Republic, universal neural-link assessments —conducted from early childhood as part of ordinary education, health monitoring, and developmental tracking — establish detailed baselines for each person's cognitive patterns. These assessments are non-invasive, consensual, and encrypted under strict constitutional privacy statutes. AGI systems scan continuously for subtle markers: unusually stable coherence in neural microtubule activity during focused attention, elevated inter-hemispheric synchronization during moments of empathy or shared intention, anomalous anticipatory signals in the default mode network before unanticipated events, or unusual kinesthetic resonance in the motor cortex during intention-focused tasks. These indicators do not guarantee the existence of special abilities but reliably point toward trainable potential with greater than 85 percent predictive accuracy across populations. Children flagged for high potential receive optional enrichment modules integrated into standard curricula, ensuring that opportunity is distributed equitably regardless of geography, socioeconomic background, or genetic lineage.

Training protocols are careful, gradual, and grounded in empirical observation rather than mysticism. They typically combine targeted mental exercises drawn from ancient contemplative traditions (refined and validated by AGI meta-analysis), real-time biofeedback from personal neural interfaces, controlled simulation environments provided by AGI-generated virtual realities, and regular periods of practice in natural, unplugged settings such as wilderness preserves or meditation gardens. The emphasis is always on ethical development, emotional maturity, and integration into a balanced life rather than raw power or competitive advantage. Citizens are encouraged to view these faculties as extensions of normal human sensitivity and cognition — akin to learning a musical instrument or mastering a sport — rather than supernatural gifts. Progress is tracked longitudinally, with AGI providing individualized coaching that adapts to each practitioner's unique neural signature. By late adolescence, a substantial portion of the population — currently around fifteen percent — demonstrates reliable access to at least one of these abilities, with many developing competence in two or more through continued voluntary practice into adulthood. Community-based "psi circles" in neighborhoods, workplaces, and colonies foster peer support, mentorship, and collective refinement, turning what was once solitary exploration into a shared cultural practice.

Telepathy, the direct sharing of thoughts, feelings, or intentions between minds, builds upon the natural human capacity for emotional resonance and unspoken understanding that has always existed in close relationships—between parents and children, spouses, or comrades in arms. Modern training refines this into controlled, consensual exchanges governed by explicit protocols. Practitioners learn to establish temporary, clearly bounded linkages that allow the flow of information while protecting deeper privacy. The experience is often described in citizen testimonies as a gentle overlapping of awareness, a warm merging of perspectives that feels both intimate and respectful, rather than intrusion or violation. In diplomatic work, telepaths have become essential members of negotiation teams. They discern genuine intentions behind formal language, especially when dealing with cultures whose emotional expressions differ markedly from our own. Their presence has repeatedly helped de-escalate potential conflicts by revealing unspoken fears, shared hopes, or hidden cultural assumptions that might otherwise have escalated into misunderstanding. Telepathic teams have proven invaluable in high-stakes negotiations with other powers, where nuances of intent can determine the difference between peaceful resolution of an international crisis and open conflict.

In military and border operations, telepathy allows units to maintain coherence and rapid coordination even when electronic communications are jammed, compromised, or cannot be used for operational security reasons. The border forces, responsible for monitoring vast territories on Earth, throughout the asteroid belt, on Mars, and around the exoplanet colonies, have found silent mind-to-mind contact particularly valuable for long-range patrols, search-and-rescue missions, and emergency response. A single telepathic operator can maintain real-time situational awareness across a squad dispersed over hundreds of kilometers, sharing not just data but the felt sense of urgency, calm, or compassion that words alone cannot convey. This capability has reduced response times in crises and strengthened unit cohesion in environments where traditional signals fail. In the arts, telepathic collaboration has opened entirely new realms of collective creativity.

Musicians, visual artists, writers, and dancers regularly engage in shared-mind sessions that produce works of unusual emotional depth and structural coherence. Audiences often describe these pieces — whether concertos performed by telepathically linked musicians or ballets performed by linked dancers — as evoking a sense of profound intimacy and coordination among the artists. These collaborative works have enriched cultural life, fostering a deeper sense of communal identity across the Republic's far-flung domains.

Remote viewing — the perception of distant or concealed locations and events — has proven equally practical and, in some domains, transformative. Trained viewers can often provide accurate, detailed descriptions of places they have never physically visited, with resolution levels that frequently exceed what would be expected from conventional intelligence gathering. AGI assists by offering immediate, objective feedback during training sessions: cross-referencing viewer reports against satellite imagery, probe data, or sealed test targets, helping practitioners distinguish clear perceptual signals from imaginative overlay or emotional projection. Viewers enter a quieted state, anchor their awareness to a coordinate vector supplied by AGI, and allow impressions to arise — visual, auditory, kinesthetic, even olfactory — before recording them in structured formats. Accuracy improves markedly with practice, and standardized protocols ensure results are verifiable and useful.

The Republic's border forces use remote viewing to monitor isolated regions and orbital approaches where physical sensors remain sparse or vulnerable to adversarial jamming. Diplomatic missions employ it to gather sensitive intelligence on host countries' infrastructure, military assets, and government operations. In scientific exploration, remote viewers have contributed valuable preliminary data about distant star systems, including exoplanet geography and climates, information later confirmed and refined by robotic probes and crewed missions. Artists have used the faculty to create powerful immersive installations that bring distant cosmic phenomena or historical sites into public awareness with striking immediacy and emotional resonance. Educational programs now incorporate remote-viewing exercises that allow students to "visit" distant worlds or ancient locations, deepening their connection to the broader universe and enhancing spatial and historical understanding.

Precognition, the direct sensing of imminent events, is perhaps the most carefully studied of these abilities because of its profound implications for decision-making, risk management, and ethical responsibility. Contemporary researchers understand it not as fixed prophecy or fatalistic destiny but as the ability to observe the branching structure of time within the six-dimensional framework of spacetime. Human consciousness appears able to launch itself along the three temporal axes as a massless observer, in a manner analogous to remote viewing. AGI assists in the development of this skill by monitoring and mapping brain activity during training sessions and adjusting training protocols as needed.

In governance and defense, precognitive practitioners serve on advisory councils, helping identify emerging risks such as solar activity, supply-chain stresses, or subtle social tensions that could escalate into unrest. Their contributions have informed policy adjustments that prevented major crises. The diplomatic corps has found advance awareness of shifting attitudes among other nations particularly useful in maintaining stable relationships and negotiating equitable agreements. In exoplanet colonization efforts, precognition aids in choosing optimal settlement sites, timing launches, and anticipating environmental challenges on new worlds. Medical researchers integrate precognitive insights with conventional epidemiology and genomic modeling to anticipate disease outbreaks or individual health vulnerabilities, dramatically improving preventive care, particularly on distant outposts where rapid evacuation is impossible. In everyday life, many citizens use these insights for personal guidance in career choices, relationships, and creative endeavors, always framed as one source of information among many.

Telekinesis, the direct influence of focused intention on physical systems, remains the most demanding faculty to develop but has produced some of the most striking empirical demonstrations. Training usually begins with microscopic or quantum-sensitive targets, where statistical effects can be measured reliably, before progressing to larger-scale influence under controlled conditions. With time, some practitioners can use telekinesis to move large objects weighing many tons. Archeologists have used these results to crack previously unsolvable mysteries, such as the question of how the Great Pyramids of Giza and the Sacsayhuaman fortress in Cuzco were built. The underlying process appears consistent with the massless consciousness model behind remote viewing and precognition. In this case directed human awareness seems able to create kinetic effects by modulating six-dimensional spacetime with remarkable efficiency. AGI systems provide precise real-time monitoring, helping practitioners achieve and sustain the necessary mental coherence without excessive strain.

Military and border applications include the remote stabilization of critical equipment during emergencies and interference with adversarial weapons systems when necessary. In construction and colonization, telekinetic operators work in partnership with robotic systems in zero-gravity or hazardous environments on Earth, achieving levels of precision and adaptability that purely mechanical approaches struggle to match. Artists have created dynamic installations and performances in which matter responds directly to collective or individual intention, producing experiences that challenge conventional distinctions between the mind and external reality. In medicine, the ability is used for non-invasive manipulation of nanoscale therapeutic agents and gentle realignment of biological tissues, offering new options for treatment in remote locations where advanced surgical facilities are unavailable.

Throughout the Republic, the employment of these revived human abilities is guided by ongoing ethical deliberation in polis assemblies. Strict consent protocols are mandatory. Privacy protections are rigorously maintained. AGI itself monitors aggregate patterns of use — not to enforce rules but to flag potential risks such as neural fatigue or unintended side effects. Citizen practitioners are encouraged to balance psi work with regular periods of unplugged time in natural environments, preserving the grounded, embodied quality of human experience. Public forums regularly debate best practices, ensuring that technological augmentation and innate human capacities operate together responsibly.

This revival of latent abilities reveals something fundamental about the relationship between AGI and human consciousness. AGI can surpass us in speed, memory, and the manipulation of symbolic information. It can design superb training protocols, analyze results with extraordinary precision, and simulate possible futures based on vast datasets. Yet it cannot replicate the direct, intuitive, first-person qualities of telepathic resonance, remote perception, precognitive apprehension, or psychokinetic influence. These capacities seem intimately tied to the specific nature of human consciousness operating within physical reality. In this sense, AGI has not replaced or diminished the human mind; it has acted as a powerful catalyst for its fuller expression.

By reclaiming these atrophied faculties, the Republic has taken a significant step toward a more complete understanding of our place in the cosmos. The old division between scientific and psychic phenomena has dissolved at long last. What emerges now is a broader naturalism — one willing to investigate all observable aspects of reality with rigor and openness. The six-dimensional spacetime framework, grounded in both mathematical elegance and empirical observation, provides a bridge between physics, consciousness studies, and lived human experience.

Challenges certainly remain. Individual differences in aptitude raise questions of fairness and opportunity that the Republic continues to address through universal access to screening and training. There are risks of psychological strain or over-dependence that require careful cultural and medical attention. Skeptical voices, though fewer than in previous centuries, still perform a valuable service by insisting on high standards of evidence and replication. Cultural integration also demands ongoing work to ensure these practices enhance rather than disrupt community life.

Nevertheless, the overall direction is clear. The American Republic has used AGI not to sideline human distinctiveness but to rediscover and cultivate it. In doing so, it honors the ancient Athenian commitment to the development of "arete" (virtue) while assisting its citizens with the highest possible development of their faculties. Telepathy strengthens communal bonds and mutual understanding. Remote viewing extends our collective field of awareness. Precognition sharpens foresight and responsible action. Telekinesis expresses the creative dialogue between mind and matter. Together, these revived capacities suggest that the human story is still unfolding—that technological progress and the deepening of our innate potentials can walk hand in hand, each enriching the other in the service of a flourishing polis.

XVIII

The Creative Arts in the Reborn Republic

In Anno Domini 2126, the American Republic extends like a living organism across the familiar continents of its birth, the icy expanses of Greenland, and outward into the lunar and Martian settlements, reaching even to colonies on twenty distant exoplanets. Universal High Income has dissolved the old shadows of material necessity, granting every citizen a material abundance once reserved for the privileged few of earlier centuries. Artificial General Intelligence and sophisticated robotics have taken on the repetitive burdens that once weighed on human hands and days, while neural technologies and the reawakening of latent perceptual capacities have opened new windows into the mysteries of consciousness. In this landscape, the creative arts have not merely survived; they have entered a profound Renaissance, one that echoes the deepest impulses of life itself — the drive toward form, expression, and connection that has animated nature since its beginnings.

The question of how habits form and evolve, not only in organisms but in human societies and polities, and in the very processes of mind, is intrinsically fascinating. What we see now in the Republic feels like a natural extension of those inquiries: a world where creativity results not from scarcity or compulsion but from an intrinsic participation in the ongoing creativity of the cosmos. Art is no longer a marginal pursuit squeezed between economic demands. It has become central to the cultivation of what the Athenians called arete—excellence, virtue, the full flowering of human potential. Citizens create because creation is how we deepen our relationship with reality, with one another, and with the greater field of awareness that seems to permeate existence. Technology serves as a collaborator and amplifier of human efforts, rather than their replacement, supporting our innate capacities rather than diminishing them.

This transformation did not take place overnight. In the turbulent decades of the 2020s and 2030s, artists still navigated the choppy waters of precarity. Many painted or composed under the pressure of markets that rewarded novelty over depth. Early forms of generative intelligence were met with understandable suspicion — tools that could produce images or texts rapidly, yet often felt disconnected from the lived, embodied rhythms of human imagination. Robotics remained largely mechanical and industrial, confined to assembly lines. Yet even then, subtle shifts were visible: the first primitive neural link technologies, growing interest in forms of perception that transcended the five senses, and a quiet recognition that consciousness might extend beyond the skull in ways that mechanistic science had long denied.

By the 2040s and 2050s, the dual emergence of reliable neural linking and Universal High Income changed everything. The necessity to sell one's work for survival evaporated. People could devote years — decades, even — to a single body of work without anxiety. What had been latent abilities, long dismissed by materialist orthodoxy, began to reappear more consistently: forms of direct knowing, influence at a distance, and shared mental states that suggested the mind is far more participatory and extended than we had been taught. AGI systems evolved into responsive presences, not mere calculators but entities capable of genuine dialogue, attuned to the subtle qualities of the human intellect. Robotics developed sensitivity and grace, becoming an extension of the body that could move with nuance and respond to emotional atmospherics. The old universities and cultural centers transformed into Virtue Enclaves, places where exploration of these capacities occurred alongside artistic training, fostering a new integration of technology, perception, and the soul.

Today, creativity permeates daily existence in the Republic. From early childhood, individuals engage with AGI companions that encourage playful experimentation with form, color, sound, and movement through immersive simulations. As they mature, people choose paths of deep artistic commitment or more occasional engagement, secure in the knowledge that their material needs are met and that service to the larger community — whether in exploration, mediation, or stewardship — arises from choice rather than coercion. Art has become both universal and aspirational. Excellence is honored through the resonance a work creates in those who experience it — the way it awakens latent potentials or strengthens the bonds of the polis.

Let us consider how the various arts are practiced today. In the visual realm, the hand and eye retain their ancient dignity. Many still spend long hours in quiet studios along Greenland's fjords or in the deserts of New Mexico, layering pigments or carving stone with the deliberate slowness that cultivates presence. Yet the majority of visual work now dances with technology in ways that feel alive. Robotic extensions, guided by neural connection, magnify the skill of painters and sculptors, allowing for movements of extraordinary precision while preserving the artist's spontaneous gestures. Those who have developed their telekinetic ability can shape materials directly with focused intention, coaxing clay or glass into forms that seem to embody the human spirit. AGI systems offer suggestions drawn from vast archives of human and natural pattern, not as directives but as invitations to dialogue — proposing harmonies of hue informed by the play of light on distant worlds or the structures of living organisms.

Imagine a large kinetic installation in a polis plaza on Earth: thousands of suspended human figures and geometrical shapes that shift and respond to the collective emotional tone of those nearby, detected through ambient neural fields. Such works never repeat themselves exactly. They become living participants in the community's life, mirroring grief with subdued motion or celebration with luminous cascades. On the Moon, coordinated swarms of autonomous units create vast murals across crater walls, composed in real time through shared awareness between distant artists and their technological partners. These works, visible from orbit, serve as reminders of our place within a vastly larger living system — a cosmic community rather than a collection of isolated entities.

Music, too, has expanded beyond its former boundaries. Neural interfaces allow composers to encounter soundscapes directly within awareness, free from the limitations of ear or instrument. Intelligent collaborators generate variations on emerging themes, while mixed human and robotic ensembles perform with tireless responsiveness, adapting to environments from zero gravity to the depths of underwater domes. Citizens share compositions through immersive archives where listeners can enter the music as participants, experiencing its structures from within.

Music has burst far beyond its traditional confines. While many musicians still cherish the intimate, physical bond of fingers on strings or keys, or lips against a mouthpiece, others now conduct performances through seamless neural links to tireless robotic avatars that never tire and can execute the most demanding passages with flawless accuracy. Some composers no longer touch an instrument at all; they shape entire symphonies entirely within their minds, where advanced neural interfaces translate thought directly into shimmering, fully realized sound.

This evolution has liberated music, transforming it into an almost boundless art form. Composers step inside living soundscapes, experiencing new sonic worlds directly in their awareness, unconstrained by ears or physical tools. Intelligent collaborators — artificial minds of extraordinary creativity — spin spontaneous variations on emerging themes, while hybrid human-robotic ensembles perform with nearly inexhaustible energy and sensitivity. These ensembles adapt fluidly to any environment, from the weightless silence of orbital concert halls to the azure stillness of underwater domes. Listeners, in turn, no longer sit passively; they step into immersive musical archives and move through the composition itself, exploring its architecture, emotions, and textures from within as active participants.

A particularly moving development involves communion with other forms of life. On certain exoplanets, musicians have learned to attune to the subtle electrochemical patterns of microbial communities, translating these into audible realms through patient listening and technological mediation. The resulting works feel less like human imposition and more like conversation across kingdoms of being. In earthly settlements, communal singing blends living voices with generated harmonics, producing evolving performances that shift with the mood of participants. Large festivals feature thousands of performers — human and robotic — moving in synchronized patterns in neoclassical plazas, their sounds carried across the polis. Such experiences often evoke a sense of participation in a greater harmony, one that echoes the ordered yet spontaneous patterns we observe throughout the natural world.

AGI has become the ultimate literary catalyst. It grants writers effortless mastery of every language known to scholarship, both ancient and modern, and fluency across every style and tradition. A 22nd-century poet might compose an epic poem describing the romance of interstellar travel and the discovery and settlement of new star systems in the rolling dactylic hexameters of Homeric Greek. A historian, guided by immersive AGI reconstructions, might craft an award-winning chronicle of the Great Transition from scarcity to abundance in the mid-21st century, written in the

American English of 2036, with all the clarity and moral force of the finest American prose.

Readers, too, have been transformed. With AGI tutors and neural-link interfaces, they can master ancient and modern languages in a fraction of the time once required, stepping directly into the linguistic and cultural worlds of the works they love. The literary experience has become infinitely richer, more intimate, and more alive for both writers and their readers. Readers interested in the history and literature of Ancient Egypt can now immerse themselves in the beauty of ancient poems and histories written in hieroglyphs. Enthusiasts of the Mayan civilization of Central America, by the same token, can immerse themselves in the inscriptions carved on enigmatic stelae, reading them as if they were written in modern English.

The performing arts have achieved remarkable vitality. Robotic dancers and actors move with superhuman fluidity yet respond to human partners with remarkable sensitivity, creating dialogues between flesh and mechanism that probe questions of identity and embodiment. Groups attuned through shared awareness choreograph pieces where emotion flows smoothly among participants, producing subtle expressions of collective feeling. Those with precognitive sensitivity can sense emerging atmospheres in an audience, allowing performances to adapt in the moment with extraordinary empathy. Performances can incorporate subtle manipulations of light and plasma, creating trails of color that respond to sentiment and intention. Theater now often blurs the line between spectator and participant; audiences linked neurally may influence unfolding events, while experiencing historical periods or philosophical encounters with uncanny vividness. These experiences do more than entertain — they cultivate the virtues necessary for a thriving interstellar society: empathy, courage, discernment, and a sense of connection across time and space.

Immersive environments represent perhaps the most fluid frontier, where creation and lived reality interpenetrate. Full-sensory neural systems and holographic technologies allow artists to shape entire worlds that communities can inhabit together. Physical spaces evolve in response to collective presence — gardens bloom according to shared mood, and structures reshape themselves gently over time. On new worlds, entire settlements are conceived as ongoing artworks, their forms emerging through participatory design.

Persistent virtual worlds exist, based upon neural link technology and AGI. There citizens can collaborate on architectural designs, engage in ethical dialogues within simulated classical settings, or explore landscapes shaped by collective dreaming. These spaces gently provoke reflection on beauty, justice, and harmony, nurturing mental and spiritual growth.

Their physical counterparts appear throughout the Republic: sculptures that convey rich emotional depth to those attuned to them, and artworks deliberately created to reveal their fullest meaning when viewed from a distance. Up close, one sees only intricate details and textures, but from afar — often through enhanced perception — the entire piece resolves into a unified whole. Patterns emerge, emotional and energetic fields become coherent, and the complete artistic intention suddenly comes alive, delivering a profound, holistic impression that cannot be grasped by examining its parts alone.

The reawakening of latent cognitive capacities has added dimensions to artistic practice that earlier eras could scarcely have imagined. In the renewed Republic, master sculptors wield telekinesis to carve stone, wood, and clay with breathtaking precision and fluidity, shaping works of immense detail that seem to breathe with living emotion. Remote viewers paint luminous canvases that capture the birth of distant stars, the swirling nebulae of new galaxies, and the intimate daily life of ancient extraterrestrial civilizations — scenes no ordinary eye has ever witnessed. Telepathic novelists craft profound narratives that explore the transformed human condition with a depth and empathy rivaling Dostoevsky, illuminating the inner struggles, joys, and moral complexities of a post-singularity society. Together, these artists create works that do more than please the senses: they expand consciousness, awaken wonder, and help citizens navigate the spiritual and ethical realities of the reborn Republic.

Questions of authenticity naturally come up in a world where art can be shaped by thought, technology, and collective minds. Yet the old fears — that machines would replace human creativity — have quietly faded away. In their place, a new reality has emerged: advanced technology and AGI have become powerful partners that unlock hidden human abilities rather than replace them.

Carefully designed protocols, shaped by open public debate, ensure that every major work still carries genuine human vision and intention at its core. To keep that human spark alive, artists regularly step away from their enhanced abilities for periods of unmediated creation, working with simple tools and unaided senses. These deliberate returns to clay, charcoal, marble, wood, and raw perception honor the beauty of imperfection and the raw thrill of direct encounter: the intimate, unfiltered experience of feeling cool clay yield beneath your fingers, struggling with a stubborn charcoal line, or seeing the grain of wood with nothing but your own eyes. It is the messy, immediate, deeply human connection between artist and material that no technology can replicate.

Challenges remain, of course. The dizzying abundance of possibilities can lead to overstimulation, so many artists retreat into untouched natural settings to rest and reconnect. New levels of sensitivity require careful training to master. And the delicate balance between individual inspiration and collective co-creation continues to be thoughtfully explored in regular community gatherings.

The deeper rewards are evident everywhere. Artistic practice has become a primary school for virtue. Painting cultivates sustained attention and humility before the materials. Music deepens the capacity for harmony and resonance with others. Writing sharpens moral imagination. Communities strengthened through shared creation develop the cohesion required for a vast, distributed society. Young people display heightened emotional range and inventive capacity. Cultural exchanges with other intelligences benefit from artistic sensitivity. Even the processes of healing and exploration are enriched: therapeutic environments incorporate sound and movement attuned to individual needs; new worlds are adorned with gardens and performance spaces that embody care and beauty from the outset.

The Republic's founding principles recognize the centrality of the arts: the polis exists to nurture human excellence, and the arts make excellence visible and palpable. As the new stage of American civilization moves into its second century, the arts serve as its animating spirit. In a universe where intelligence can simulate countless realities and machines can realize almost any form, humanity continues to choose the heartfelt act of creation. This fusion of ancient perceptual wisdom with emerging technologies has yielded not cold perfection but living, evolving beauty, full of surprise, mystery, and love.

For the creative impulse is woven into the fabric of existence itself. In choosing to create, we align with the deeper habits of a participatory cosmos.

Every citizen, in some measure, becomes an artist. Seen from this perspective, the entire Republic is a work in progress — expansive, responsive, and ever more fully alive. As new colonies take root and fresh worlds open to human exploration, the scope and scale of human creation expand as well in a continuous renaissance.

This renaissance invites us to reconsider our place within nature. Creativity is not a human invention imposed upon a mechanical universe but a manifestation of the universe's own creative nature, manifesting in humanity and its creations with particular clarity. In recovering and extending our capacities — technological, perceptual, communal — we rediscover something primordial: the joy of shaping form in conscious relationship with the world around us. The arts in this age remind us that we are not separate observers but active participants in a living cosmos full of memory, called to contribute our unique voices to its resonant symphony.

XIX

A Day in the Life of the Polis

The first light of an early September dawn filtered through the tall windows of the Thompson family home in Atlanta's restored Inman Park neighborhood. Ancient Victorian houses with their ornate gingerbread trim stood shoulder to shoulder with graceful new buildings whose lines followed gentle curves inspired by the mathematics of spacetime itself. The year was 2126. The United States had become the interstellar Republic: a vast federation based on direct democracy, Universal High Income, and material prosperity so complete that scarcity existed only in history texts. Artificial general intelligence and billions of humanoid robots had eliminated drudgery, while the economy hummed along at ten to twelve percent annual growth. In Georgia, one of the original fifty states, daily life moved to the ancient rhythm of otium — the refined, civilized leisure once prized by the Athenians, and now available to every citizen.

For the Thompson family the day began as most days did: quietly, purposefully, and peacefully. Elias Thompson, forty-two, tall and bearded, with the powerful forearms and callused hands of a working sculptor, woke first. His internal chronometer, synchronized with the household AGI they affectionately called Curie, eased him from sleep at 6:45 a.m. No harsh alarm disturbed the peace of the house. Instead, the bedroom walls brightened to a soft golden hue, and a delicate scent of pine and citrus drifted through the air, drawn from the family's preference profile. Sophia, thirty-nine, murmured beside him, her dark hair spread across the pillow, one arm still draped across his chest. "Five more minutes," she whispered, smiling with her eyes still closed. Elias kissed her forehead, rose, and felt the floor tiles warm instantly beneath his bare feet.

The house itself was comfortable rather than ostentatious—a four-bedroom home with self-cleaning surfaces, holographic walls capable of displaying any work of art, or a vista from Earth or the colonies, and a modest garden maintained by a dedicated robot named Oak. It was "modest" only by the standards of a civilization where abundance had become the baseline. Elias stretched, then walked quietly down the hall.

Curie orchestrated the children's awakening with gentle precision. Fifteen-year-old Lila's room overlooked the neighborhood sports center. Her walls shimmered into a holographic forest canopy as her tutor, Eos, greeted her in a calm, melodic voice. "Good morning, Lila. Today's curriculum thread examines polis ethics through Socratic dialogue. Shall we begin the day with your preferred stretch sequence?" Lila groaned theatrically, pulled the light sheet over her head for one defiant moment, then rolled out of bed with the fluid grace of a born athlete. At fifteen she already balanced demanding studies with serious training in zero-gravity dance, attending weekly sessions linked by warp relay to instructors on the Martian colony. She slipped into a smart-fabric athletic suit that adjusted its compression to her biometrics and padded downstairs.

Ten-year-old Theo bounded out of his room moments later, his walls alive with a feed from the Atlanta Hawks' training camp. "Curie, did Atlanta win last night?" he asked, voice bright with anticipation. The AGI confirmed the victory and played a crisp holographic replay, complete with commentary on the final sequence. Theo's AGI tutor, Helix, reminded him that the morning mathematics module would involve modeling warp-drive trajectories — making Riemannian geometry feel like an exciting game rather than abstract theory.

Five-year-old Mira was last. She toddled into the hallway in pajamas that shifted colors according to her mood—soft pastels this morning. Her tutor, Lark, sang a gentle welcome song while a small, Optimus robot assistant helped her dress. Mira's education remained pure delight: stories interwoven with basic geometry, sensory exploration with real materials, and long stretches of unstructured play.

By 7:30 a.m. the family had converged in the sunlit kitchen. Breakfast was never rushed; it was a collaborative ritual. The household fabricator, limited by law to safe domestic scale, produced warm sourdough loaves from heirloom grains Elias had sourced from a cooperative in the Georgia countryside. Sophia activated the coffee station; rich beans from long-established Latin American partners filled the air with aroma as milk frothed under precise temperature control. Eggs from the family's own backyard chickens — still a cherished luxury — sizzled gently. Real ceramic plates and hand woven cloth napkins graced the table, small but meaningful assertions of human craftsmanship in an age of perfect fabrication.

Conversation moved easily across the table. Elias spread butter from former France on his toast and asked Lila about her upcoming sortition selection for the neighborhood youth council. "They're debating interstellar migration quotas this session," he said. Lila's eyes brightened. "I want to argue for more spots for Earth families," she replied. "Not everyone has visited the colonies yet. We need balance." Theo chimed in, asking whether he could help sand the latest shipment of rare woods and stone in the workshop after breakfast. Mira, perched on her booster seat, demanded her favorite story about "the stars that sing," drawn from actual logs of early warp expeditions. Sophia laughed, her practical ponytail swinging, and promised they would film a family fitness segment later that incorporated Mira's enthusiastic but chaotic dance moves.

After breakfast, the day branched into its natural rhythms, supported by the polis's invisible infrastructure of abundance. Elias kissed Sophia and the children and stepped into the large workshop attached to the rear of the house. Thompson Sculptural Studio was his small business and creative sanctuary. He employed three apprentices — Marcus, Thomas, and young Michael — all in their twenties, men who had chosen the demanding satisfactions of craftsmanship over pure leisure. The workshop smelled of stone dust, linseed oil, and the faint metallic tang of precision tools. Rare woods and blocks of stone arrived weekly via autonomous hyperloop from carefully managed Earth forests and quarries or from bio-engineered groves on distant colonies.

Today's major commission dominated the space: a life-sized marble statue of the Virgin Mary for the local Catholic church. The massive block of pure white Carrara marble had arrived the previous week, its surface still bearing the faint marks of the quarrying process. Elias approached it with the reverence of a man who understood both material and meaning. He had already studied dozens of historical renderings and contemporary devotional art, but the final vision was his own—serene, spiritual, and timeless.

His hands moved with practiced grace as he guided the robotic chisels. The apprentices handled the initial heavy blocking with powerful robotic assists that still required human judgment for every critical decision. "Feel the stone," Elias instructed Marcus, placing the younger man's hands on the marble. “See how the natural veins here could become the flow of her robes. Respect what the material wants to become.” They discussed proportion, gesture, and emotional resonance while a small drone hovered nearby, projecting holographic reference models and precise measurements. No wages beyond Universal High Income changed hands; the workshop operated as a micro-cooperative, with modest profits contributing to the national dividend. By mid-morning they had roughed out the major forms—the gentle tilt of the head, the protective curve of the arms, the cascading folds of drapery. Elias stepped back, wiped stone dust from his forehead, and studied the emerging figure with quiet satisfaction. As usual, he would work for six hours today, leaving ample time for family and the evening town hall.

Meanwhile, Sophia had transformed the lower level of the home into her professional fitness studio. Her platform, CurvatureFit, reached millions of viewers across Earth and the colonies. She blended intense physical training with mindfulness practices drawn from the polis emphasis on balanced living. Dressed in a smart-suit that tracked every biometric marker and adjusted resistance in real time, she recorded a forty-five-minute “Otium Flow” session tailored for parents. Bodyweight movements, light free weights forged from asteroid alloys, and guided breathing exercises filled the hour. “In the polis,” she said to the holographic camera with a warm smile, sweat glistening on her skin, “fitness is not about survival or appearance. It is about celebrating the body that carries your mind and soul.” Live comments poured in from a temperate exoplanet colony and from viewers in Earth regions adopting elements of the American cultural model.

The children’s morning continued with natural energy. Lila joined a virtual debate club at the collegiate level, arguing the proper role of AGI advisory councils in interstellar policy. Theo and two neighborhood friends enjoyed a lesson in Riemannian geometry, exploring the magic of multidimensional manifolds with the aid of their AGI tutors and neural links. Afterward several hours they moved on to reading the Odyssey in Homeric Greek. Mira remained closer to home, exploring the garden with her robotic aide while Lark guided her through gentle lessons on botany and genetics.

Lunch at 12:30 p.m. brought everyone together again beneath the garden’s shaded pergola. Fresh salads, perfectly prepared steaks, and sweet exotic fruits from the exoplanets covered the table. Elias described the morning’s progress on the Virgin Mary statue; Sophia shared touching viewer stories from her holographic stream, including a family in the former EU territories experimenting with sortition. The children recounted their activities with enthusiasm. No one watched the clock with dread. Each person offered one thing they were grateful for: Mira's was "the singing stars," Theo's "helping Dad with the marble," Lila's "debating ideas with friends across light-years."

The afternoon deepened the day's engagement. Elias returned to the workshop for two more focused hours, refining the statue's facial expression and the delicate drapery that would convey compassion and tenderness. Sophia edited her morning footage, adjusting pacing for colonial audiences who lived under slightly different gravity, then recorded a short collaborative yoga sequence with Mira that turned into delighted laughter and play. Lila volunteered at the local archive, curating stories from both Earth and the colonies for public access. Theo competed in a chess tournament linked by a quantum connection with players on Proxima Centauri b. Mira napped peacefully, then painted with natural pigments at a small outdoor easel.

By four o'clock the family walked together to the neighborhood stadium, a graceful structure echoing classical structures. Youth track and field practice filled the field with athletic energy. Lila sprinted against friends, her form analyzed instantly by trackside AGI coaches that offered encouragement rather than commands. Theo hurled the javelin, laughing as it flew farther than the day before. Mira toddled along the sidelines, cheered by parents and a handful of humanoid assistants who provided water and towels but never overshadowed the human joy of competition. In the polis, sport remained community glue—embodying the ancient ideal of mens sana in corpore sano.

Dinner at 6:30 p.m. was the day's warm center. Elias lit the outdoor grill with mesquite, filling the air with fragrant smoke. Sophia and the children prepared vegetables and sides. The table held grilled sausages and burgers from local cooperatives, fresh bread, and a dessert made from heirloom cacao from African partners. Conversation turned richer. Elias read aloud a passage on theosis from Saint Gregory Palamas, a text experiencing renewed interest in the spiritual renaissance made possible by material security. Though the Thompsons were Catholic, not Orthodox, they drew freely from the broader revival of religious and philosophical inquiry. Lila asked eager questions about the latest news from the exoplanet frontier. Curie projected a holographic star map showing the growing web of interstellar trade routes that now carried fifteen percent of the rapidly growing U.S. GDP.

Evening otium followed naturally. In the living room, with walls displaying the Atlanta skyline at dusk and the faint lights of orbital habitats on the horizon, Theo practiced guitar on a hand-crafted instrument. Mira stacked blocks into increasingly complex geometric forms that revealed an intuitive grasp of spatial relationships. Sophia reviewed her metrics for the day — another strong viewership day — and answered thoughtful messages from followers. Elias sketched ideas for a new series of smaller devotional pieces inspired by Byzantine art. No one labored beyond chosen hours. The remainder of the evening belonged to family, reflection, and quiet preparation for tomorrow's local assembly.

By ten o'clock bedtime rituals began. Curie dimmed the lights and played soft ambient music drawn from natural soundscapes across the federation. Teeth were brushed with smart brushes that offered gentle health insights. Stories were read — Mira with real paper books, the older children with interactive holographic tales. Hugs lingered. Elias and Sophia retreated to their bedroom, reviewing polis news: steady economic expansion, new trade agreements, and updates from citizen oversight boards monitoring AGI alignment. They spoke softly of their blessings — the freedom to do meaningful work, to raise children without financial anxiety, and to live as full citizens of a prosperous interstellar civilization.

Lights out by 10:30 p.m. The house settled into quiet efficiency. Robotic systems performed overnight maintenance while Curie monitored gently. Outside, Atlanta hummed with the low sound of hyperloops and distant cheers from a professional baseball game. Across fifty states and twenty colonies, millions of families experienced their own versions of this day.

For the Thompsons, the Tuesday had been entirely unremarkable — precisely why it mattered so deeply. In the reborn polis, an average day stood as quiet proof that technology had not supplanted humanity but had elevated it. Universal High Income had removed the ancient fear of want. Humanoid robots and AGI managed drudgery, freeing every citizen to sculpt marble into sacred beauty, to teach fitness as celebration, to debate ethics across light-years, to run on sunlit tracks, or simply to chase fireflies through a summer garden. The ancient Athenian ideals of direct participation, creative excellence, and balanced living had scaled successfully to an interstellar federation without losing their essence.

As Elias drifted toward sleep with Sophia's hand resting in his, he felt the same serene certainty that had defined the American experiment since the AGI breakthroughs a century ago: the hours once stolen by necessity now belonged fully to the self, the family, the community, and the soul's patient quest for meaning amid superabundance. Tomorrow would bring another ordinary miracle. He and his fellow citizens would greet it together.

XX

The Eternal Frontier and the Rebirth of the Pioneering Spirt

In the spring of 2051, as the first warp bubble enveloped the starship Argo and the blue curve of Earth fell away like a dream, something eternal and vital stirred in the American soul. The ship's maiden voyage to Proxima Centauri b was not merely a technological triumph; it was the reopening of a frontier that had been declared closed for more than a century and a half. The frontier spirit — born on the Atlantic beaches in 1607, forged across the Appalachians, the Mississippi, the Rockies, and the Pacific — had lain dormant since Frederick Jackson Turner delivered his famous 1893 address declaring the American West settled. For generations, that restless, self-reliant, optimistic energy had found no adequate outlet. The closing of the continental frontier had channeled it into industry, innovation, and eventually into the digital and corporate realms of the twentieth and early twenty-first centuries. Yet something essential had been lost. The nation grew wealthier but, in the eyes of many, softer, more bureaucratic, more inward-looking. The advent of interstellar travel, made possible by the convergence of Riemannian AGI, the Universal High Income (UHI) revolution, and breakthroughs in theoretical physics, did more than expand America's physical boundaries. It reignited the frontier spirit with astonishing brilliance, transforming it from historical memory into a permanent, defining characteristic of the American psyche. By 2126, with twenty exoplanet states in the Union and humanity's first interstellar civilization firmly established, the United States had become a nation of eternal pioneers — Homo explorans — for whom the stars were not a destination but a destiny.

The intellectual seeds of this revival were planted decades earlier, in the chaotic 2020s, long before the UHI Act or the full flowering of AGI. Serious research into interstellar propulsion began in earnest in 2036, enabled by the same advanced artificial general intelligence systems that had upended the labor market and made UHI economically feasible. What galvanized the effort was the rediscovery of an obscure but seminal 2025 book titled Faster Than Light. Written by an independent scholar working outside the mainstream academic establishment, the work had been largely ignored at publication, dismissed as speculative fringe science. Yet as Riemannian AGI systems — built on curved manifolds that mirrored the subtle geometry of human thought and the structure of the universe itself— began to comb through humanity's entire scientific literature with unprecedented depth and intuition, the book's insights rose to the surface like a long-submerged continent.

The breakthrough was elegant in its simplicity and revolutionary in its implications. Traditional proposals for faster-than-light travel, most notably the Alcubierre Drive first described in 1994, had always foundered on the same insurmountable obstacle: the requirement for exotic matter possessing negative energy density in quantities equivalent to the mass of Jupiter. No known physics could produce or stabilize such material. Faster Than Light proposed a radical synthesis. By leveraging the mathematics of three-dimensional time, treating time not as a single linear dimension but as a manifold with its own curvature, the book proposed that Alcubierre warp bubbles could be formed through the manipulation of temporal curvature alone, without the need for exotic matter. The Alcubierre drive, which contracts spacetime ahead of a vessel and expands it behind, became an engineering problem rather than a mere theoretical possibility. Causality remained inviolate, the ship never locally exceeding the speed of light within the warp bubble, and effective superluminal travel became feasible.

This theoretical foundation provided the blueprint for practical development. SpaceX, already the dominant force in near-Earth and interplanetary spaceflight thanks to its reusable launch systems and visionary leadership, took the lead. With UHI freeing vast human and financial resources from the old constraints of survival labor, the company—now operating as a public-private partnership with the recently formed Space Force—poured AGI-augmented engineering into the Argo project. The starship was completed in 2051: a sleek vessel, just 50 meters in length, capable of carrying a crew of two dozen scientists and engineers and their equipment. On its maiden voyage to Proxima Centauri b, the journey took just thirty-one days. Guided by AGI navigation systems that anticipated temporal fluctuations with sub-second precision, the Argo slipped into warp, its crew watching the stars streak into rainbow ribbons outside the viewports.

Those pioneers embodied the rebirth of the frontier spirit in flesh and blood. They were not conscripts or corporate employees but volunteers — engineers who had spent years mastering quantum-temporal field dynamics, biologists trained to study the flora and fauna of alien worlds, and geologists ready to analyze the substance, structure, and resources of newly discovered planets. Self-reliant to a degree unmatched since the nineteenth-century wagon trains, they carried the tools of survival and creation in their own hands and minds. Mid-flight, when minor instabilities appeared in the warp bubble, the engineers did not wait for ground control; they tweaked the field parameters in real time, drawing on the intuitive, sparse-reasoning capabilities of their onboard Riemannian AGI. Upon arrival, the settlers stepped onto the surface of Proxima Centauri b with the same mixture of awe and practicality that had characterized Lewis and Clark on their voyage of discovery across the vast domain of Jefferson's Louisiana Purchase. When the Argo returned to Earth, it left behind a small outpost of explorers. Within five Earth years, the outpost had become a thriving base, the first American settlement among the stars.

The symbolism was deliberate and powerful. The ship's name — Argo — evoked the original Argonauts who sailed with Jason to distant Colchis in search of the Golden Fleece. Like that mythic voyage, the interstellar journey was not one of conquest or plunder. It was the extension of humanity's exploratory drive across the ultimate ocean: the deep space between the stars. The pioneers were modern Argonauts, with a difference: seeking not treasure but new homes, new knowledge, and the sense of infinite possibilities that had always defined the American character. Their success proved that the frontier spirit had never truly died; it had merely been waiting for a frontier worthy of it.

The establishment of more colonies followed with breathtaking speed. Feasible interstellar flight, made possible by the AGI-optimized Alcubierre warp drive, turned what had once been the realm of science fiction into a practical instrument for migration and exploration. Millions of Americans — young families seeking room to breathe, young couples drawn by the promise of homesteading, scientists hungry for new knowledge, entrepreneurs envisioning entire industries on virgin worlds — boarded the growing fleet of starships. Terraforming proceeded rapidly thanks to the same AGI and robotics that had revolutionized Earth. Atmospheric processors, seeded by robotic swarms, transformed barren rocks into habitable paradises within decades. As each colony's population reached 100,000, it was granted territorial status under the U.S. Constitution. Upon hitting one million souls, it became a full state with voting representation in Congress. By 2126, twenty exoplanet states had joined the Union. The Moon and Mars, long since fully integrated, formed the inner solar system core. The United States had become humanity's first true interstellar civilization, its territory spanning light-years and its population growing rapidly.

This physical expansion reignited the frontier spirit like a prairie fire, with a force that astonished even the most optimistic analysts. Long dormant after the closing of the Western frontier in the 1890s — when the Census Bureau officially declared the American West settled — the spirit flared up in the 2050s like a long-banked fire suddenly given oxygen. Interstellar exploration and colonization became the great outlet for the most adventuresome and heroic citizens. Young men and women who might once have joined the military, started tech companies, or pursued extreme sports now trained for the colonies. They learned to live in low-gravity environments, to repair warp-field generators with their own hands, and to negotiate alien biospheres using the advanced reasoning and knowledge that AGI made possible. The same American self-reliance that had built log cabins in Kentucky in the 1800s now built pressurized habitats under alien suns. The same optimism that had driven wagon trains across the Great Plains now terraformed new worlds.

Crucially, the revival was not limited to a small cadre of elites or adventurers. Because UHI had severed the link between work and survival and ushered in an age of abundance, ordinary citizens could afford to take the risks that true pioneering demanded. A stone carver from Ohio could sell his Earthside home — now rendered luxurious by robotic construction — and use the proceeds plus his growing UHI stipend to fund passage for his family to a new exoplanet state. A teacher from California could volunteer for the first wave of educators on a newly terraformed world, knowing her income was secure. The frontier spirit became democratized on a scale Turner could never have imagined. It permeated the national psyche. Children grew up hearing stories not of the Oregon Trail but of the Proxima Centauri Run. Popular culture — holographic epics, polis debates, even children's education —

celebrated the revived pioneer virtues: courage, ingenuity, cooperation, and an unquenchable thirst for the unknown.

Philosophers and theologians, freed by otium to contemplate the deeper meanings of existence, developed new theories centered on the idea of "Homo explorans" as the natural successor to Homo sapiens. In the pre-interstellar era, humanity had been defined by its intelligence — "sapiens," Latin for "the wise one." Intelligence, both artificial and biological, had been seen as the pinnacle of existence. Now with abundance secured and the road to the stars opened, a new purpose emerged. Exploration itself became the primary telos of human life. Intelligence — whether human intuition enriched by otium or AGI's curved manifolds — was now seen as a supporting function, a tool in service of the greater drive to know, settle, and create. Theologians and philosophers across traditions found resonance in this vision. Christian thinkers spoke of interstellar travel as a means to understand the mind of God by exploring the glories of His creation. Jewish scholars drew parallels with Exodus. Even secular humanists embraced the concept, arguing that Homo explorans represented the fullest realization of human potential: not merely surviving or even thriving, but endlessly expanding into higher states of being.

This philosophical shift found its most succinct and powerful expression in a reminted Latin adage. Cicero's ancient declaration "Vivere est cogitare" — to live is to think — was reborn as "Vivere est explorare" — to live is to explore. The phrase captured the new American consensus with elegant brevity. It became the official motto of the reorganized and expanded Space Force, etched on every starship, every orbital station, every exoplanet's coat of arms, even the Great Seal of the President. Recruits swore their oaths beneath it. Schoolchildren learned it as the guiding principle of the Republic. It encapsulated the conviction that the frontier would never close again. There would always be another star, another world, another horizon calling to the restless American spirit. The Age of Exploration had not ended with Magellan or Lewis and Clark; it had only paused, waiting for the right technological and moral moment to revive on an interstellar scale. And that moment had finally arrived.

Economists and demographers were quick to quantify what the pioneers felt intuitively. As the population of the colonized worlds grew and their number multiplied, the off-Earth portion of the Republic's economy and population would one day vastly exceed the terrestrial portion. Early projections in the 2060s already showed exponential growth in the off-Earth population. The interstellar economy — driven by new resources, novel industries, and the creative energies unleashed by otium — would one day exceed Earth's output. Rare isotopes mined from asteroid belts and exoplanets, pharmaceuticals synthesized under alien gravities, cultural exports from worlds where human art blended with alien landscapes and materials — all flowed back through interstellar trade routes to enrich the Republic as a whole. The frontier had always been an economic engine; now it was an interstellar one, promising growth without end.

Political scientists speculated about yet deeper implications. The addition of exoplanet states to the Union revived and expanded the federal system in ways the Founders could scarcely have imagined. Each new state brought unique perspectives shaped by its environment — low-gravity cultures on Mars, high-radiation adaptations on certain exoplanets, communal governance experiments on still others. The polis, already thriving on Earth, adapted seamlessly to interstellar distances through AGI-mediated assemblies and neural-linked referenda. Yet the frontier spirit injected a decentralizing force. New states, populated by the most self-reliant citizens, often pushed for greater local autonomy, echoing the old Western territories' demands for statehood on their own terms. Congress debated issues unimaginable in the terrestrial era: planetary water rights, the management of AGI-augmented biospheres, and the balance between planetary sovereignty and Republic-wide defense needs. The frontier spirit thus kept the Republic dynamic, preventing the sclerosis that had afflicted older states.

Demographers foresaw a future in which the population of the Republic would be numbered in the billions — perhaps tens of billions — spread across dozens of worlds. With UHI removing economic barriers to family formation and interstellar migration providing endless living space, fertility rates stabilized at healthy levels. The old Malthusian fears evaporated. Humanity would not crowd a single planet into collapse; it would bloom across the galaxy like wildflowers after rain. The frontier spirit ensured that this growth would be vigorous and optimistic rather than cramped and fearful.

By 2126, nearly a century after the UHI Act had first made abundance possible, the revival of the frontier spirit stood as one of the Second American Revolution's most enduring legacies. The United States was no longer a continental power with space outposts; it was an interstellar civilization whose citizens carried the pioneer ethos in their bones. Children on Proxima Centauri b learned the same lessons of self-reliance that their ancestors had learned on the Kansas prairie. Families on newly settled worlds faced the same challenges — and felt the same exhilaration — as the first settlers at Jamestown or Plymouth. Some scholars, influenced by Virgil's Aeneid, asserted that America's true destiny was "imperium sine fine."

For in the end, the greatest gift of interstellar travel was not the new worlds themselves, nor even the unimaginable wealth they generated. It was the restoration of purpose. For too long, the closing of the frontier had left a void in the national soul — a quiet yearning for horizons that no longer existed. The Argo and its successors filled that void with an infinity of possibility. They reminded Americans that they were, at their core, a people defined not by comfort but by the courage to venture forth. "Vivere est explorare" was more than a motto. It was a covenant with the future: that so long as there were stars, there would be Americans striving to reach them.

The frontier spirit had returned, and it would never sleep again. In the quiet moments between warp jumps, as new suns rose over fresh horizons, the pioneers of 2126 could look back across the centuries and know that Turner had been wrong. The frontier had never truly closed. It had only been waiting for America to grow worthy of it once again.

www.ingramcontent.com/pod-product-compliance
Ingram Content Group UK Ltd.
Pitfield, Milton Keynes, MK11 3LW, UK
UKHW052023141026
15794UKWH00028B/147/J